THOSE WHO DARED

THOSE WHO DARED

EDITED BY RICHARD NELSSON

guardianbooks

Published by Guardian Books 2009

2 4 6 8 10 9 7 5 3 1

Photo credits: p. 41 Amundsen in the Antarctic: the *Guardian*; p. 59 Desert palms, Egypt by Denis Thorpe: the *Guardian*; p. 83 Wilfrid Thesiger, 1990, by Jane Bown: the *Observer*; p. 103 A jungle explorer, circa 1930: the *Guardian*; p. 137 The Matterhorn above Zermatt by Kenneth Saunders: the *Guardian*; p. 199 JRL Anderson, 1966: the *Guardian*; p. 231 Hubert Latham flies a monoplane in a gale, Blackpool, 1909, by Walter Doughty: the *Guardian*

First published in Great Britain in 2009 by
Guardian Books
Kings Place, 90 York Way
London N1 9GU

www.guardianbooks.co.uk

A CIP catalogue record for this book is available from the British Library

ISBN 978-0-85265-142-1

Typeset by seagulls.net

Printed and bound in Great Britain by Clays Ltd, St Ives PLC

CONTENTS

Introduction 1

1. Polar 7

2. Deserts 53

3. Jungles 93

4. Mountains 133

5. Oceans 183

6. Air 215

References 245

Index 246

Acknowledgments

Thanks to Lisa Darnell and Helen Brooks at Guardian Books, Mike McNay, Stephanie Cross, Mariam Yamin from the Guardian News & Media archive, and everyone in the Guardian and Observer Research & Information department. Last but not least, thanks to Fiona, Hannah and Freya for letting me embark on this adventure in the papers' archives.

Richard Nelsson
August 2009

INTRODUCTION

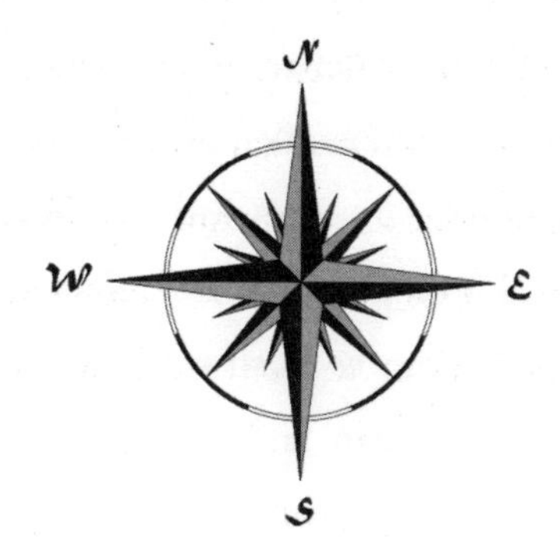

Why do it? 'Because it's there,' George Mallory answered in 1923, while he was planning his third expedition to Everest. Neat, except that it seems these shining words may have been put into his mouth by a *New York Times* reporter. The following year Mallory died on Everest and still no one knows whether or not he reached the summit.

'Because it's there' could stand not just as Mallory's epitaph but as the motive for hundreds of adventures on mountains, on the oceans, in deserts and jungles, and in the air. What else did Scott of the Antarctic die for? Or his 19th century predecessor John Franklin, who tried to navigate the North-West Passage, fabled at least since 1497 when Henry VII sent John Cabot to sort out the route which would liberate trade with the far east? A stream of English navigators followed over the centuries. Franklin died in 1845, but Roald Amundsen succeeded with a three-year navigation of the route starting in 1903. It's still not a practicable route, but the melting icecap could sort that out soon.

'God, this is an awful place,' Scott entered in his diary when he reached the South Pole in 1911, possibly because Amundsen had been first there too, and left the evidence by planting the Norwegian flag. Scott's five-man party had manhandled their sledges across the ice from the base camp, but Amundsen's team was clad in Eskimo gear instead of heavy wool, and had used fleet skis and willing dogs, some of which finished up according to plan as fresh meat. What an unBritish cad. Today we'd call it professionalism, and Amundsen himself argued pointedly, if a trifle smugly: 'Victory awaits him who has everything in order – luck, people call it. Defeat is certain for him who has neglected to take the necessary precautions in time; this is called bad luck.'

Neil Armstrong and Buzz Aldrin would have understood that. They took their stroll on the moon backed by a massive team of scientists, enough dollars to refloat many broken banks and lost bonuses, and all the technological expertise available at the time assembled under the watchful eye of Wernher von Braun, Hitler's wizard rocket builder 'liberated' by the Americans. Give or take the odd scoop of moon sand, the astronauts were closer to the the spirit of Mallory and Scott than they were to the late 18th century botanist, Sir Joseph Banks, or the Victorian biologists, Charles Darwin and Alfred Russel Wallace.

Banks had travelled with Captain Cook on his voyages, bringing back detailed notes and illustrations from Australia and South America as well as a Tahitian, Omai, whom Banks introduced into London society and procured a portrait of him by Sir Joshua Reynolds; when Omai left soon after on another of Cook's tours, the Theatre Royal, Covent Garden, produced a play for the Christmas 1785 season called *Omai – a Voyage Round the World*, a precursor of a 21st century celebrity docudrama.

Darwin and Wallace independently explored South America, Australasia, and the Malayan archipelago and, independently again, arrived at the theory of the natural selection of the species. Wallace was first in making the announcement. He was suffering a fever in the Moluccas in 1858 when he arrived at the theory and dispatched it post haste to Down, England, the name of Darwin's house near Biggin Hill. It arrived and jolted Darwin into his own fever of drafting his own closely similar theory which he had funked publishing for fear of ridicule. The book, of course, was *On the Origin of the Species.* No other travels before or since have broadened so many minds as these.

Already European nations had set out to stake a claim on the 'unknown' areas of the world; the British, especially after the loss of the American colonies, turned energetically to colouring in the white areas of the map pink. The wealthy leisured class of the mid-19th century, peaking with the Edwardians, began to explore far flung regions solely for exploration's sake and to conquer all the highest mountains of Europe. From this point until the conquest of Everest by Norgay Tenzing and Edmund Hillary in 1953, it was the challenge that excited the pursuit, not intellectual curiosity, and from the balloon flight by Jean-François Pilâtre de Rozier and François Laurent d'Arlandes, soaring over the rooftops of Paris in the balloon designed by the Montgolfier brothers, to the conquest of the moon, in the militaristic vocabulary we apply to this sort of venture, these explorers set out in a spirit not far from the public school ethic inculcated at Dr Arnold's Rugby. The two flights, by balloon and by moon rocket, were punctuated by the early days of powered flight, Blériot across the Channel, Lindbergh over the Atlantic, and Amy Johnson to Australia, and by at least one mass air race, in 1911. It started in Paris disastrously with three deaths, and proceeded to farce in the leg around Britain when these string and canvas aircraft fell out of the sky like clay pigeons, 17 of them. Only three made it as far as Edinburgh, but nobody died.

None of the pilots was quoted; perhaps they were in shock, but the gentleman amateur's approach demanded the laconic manner, however bogus. 'Dr Livingstone I presume?' Stanley remarked, though only by his own widely accepted account, which may be as suspect as Malory's three words: Livingstone was the true amateur, seeking in due time the source of the Nile; Stanley, the journalist, had in mind a pressing engagement to write a book.

We know from Scott's journal that Oates said as he left the tent and walked out into the blizzard, 'I am just going outside and may be some time.' Armstrong's remark when Aldrin joined him on the moon is unquestioned, because millions around the world heard him say, like any tourist arriving in Venice for the first time, 'Isn't that something?' But what the official history records is Armstrong's words before Aldrin disembarked: 'That's one small step for [a] man, one giant leap for mankind'. It was, of course, scripted and preordained for the history books. Armstrong stumbled and missed out the 'a' so

Wernher von Braun's Florida spinmeisters inserted it for him and now it is the truth.

'No other great adventure was as great as this,' said a leader in the following morning's *Guardian* (see below). True, but it also fell into a class of expeditions whose primary purpose was political, in this case with a background of the cold war. The United States had been shaken by the Soviet success with Gagarin's spaceflight, and President Kennedy bent every nerve to ensure that Americans should surpass this achievement. Frigid messages of congratulation passed from one power block to the other on each occasion, but the USSR couldn't bite back the sour observation that moon rock could be picked up by robot (something they then went on to prove).

Just so had Everest been conquered on May 29 1953 by a British team accompanied by the journalist James Morris, who outwitted the rest of the press by dispatching a coded message to the *Times*, and the *Times* splashed with it on Elizabeth II's coronation day, June 2. It was a last hurrah for the British empire, even though the summit was attained, not by the expedition's leader, John Hunt (Marlborough and Sandhurst), but by a New Zealander (Tuakau primary school and Auckland grammar), and a Nepalese sherpa of no known formal education.

The *Guardian* has played its own small part in the great game. It was half-seriously held that nobody who hoped to get on in his journalistic career would go anywhere in Alastair Hetherington's time as editor (1956-75) unless he was prepared to don walking boots and scale the lake district fells with the boss. The famously eccentric assistant editor and self appointed yachting editor, John Anderson, led a *Guardian* boat across the

Atlantic, spectacles Elastoplasted to his head, following the supposed route of the pre-Columbian Vikings; and the paper sponsored an endeavour by the author of *Lord of the Flies*, William Golding, to sail to Greece, but his craft sank under him two days out of Shoreham. His laconic comment is not recorded, but he is understood to have been miffed.

This is rich territory, but in the end that leading article was surely right in saying that the Apollo 22 moon landing was the greatest adventure. It should be remembered though (indeed, Tim Radford does in the final piece in this book) that in the end, the success of the expedition and the lives of Aldrin and Armstrong hung on whether they could carry out a vital repair with the end of a felt-tip pen.

Mike McNay

ONE

POLAR

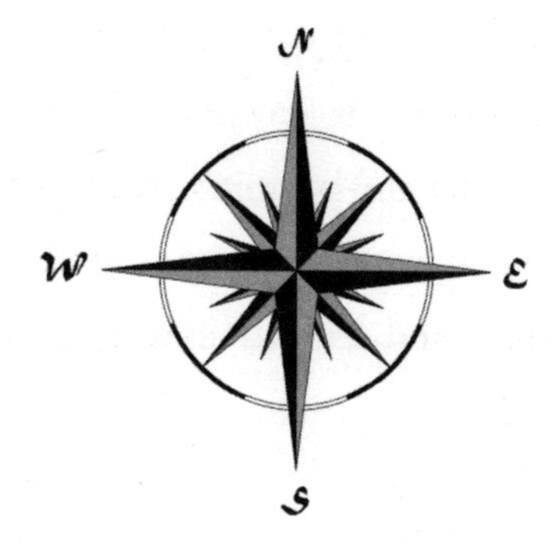

Expedition to the north pole

Observer, March 30 1818

The vessels equipped for the northern expedition are expected to sail from Deptford next week. May they return safely and successfully! That they will bring home considerable additions to the stock of useful & exalting knowledge may be reasonably hoped; and this alone is sufficient to justify the enterprise. To aim at a more perfect knowledge of the world in which we are placed, may be considered as one of the duties of those who are qualified by previous advances to search for such attainments.

Supposing the polar basin to be passable by vessels purposely equipped for the discovery, is such a passage one of which merchants ships can be prepared to avail themselves? Can such routes to given spots, though they be the nearest, be also the best, or those which vessels will ever take, except for purposes of curiosity? Will the mere chance of saving distance, at the risk of losing months, lead ordinary navigators to the regions, where

'Pale suns unfelt, at distance roll away,

And on the impassive ice the lightnings play?'*

That it will not, is no reason against the expeditions; but it is due to the enterprising men now about to leave us, to acknowledge what it is that ought not to be expected of them, to ascertain what is success, and to prevent it from being considered as a failure.

On the expedition to the north pole

Extracted from a French Paper, March 30 1818

Some English writers have already indulged themselves in illusory conjectures on this enterprise; they describe Greenland as bursting from the icy barrier which surrounds it. They repeat the traditionary reports of the last century respecting some whale ships said to have reached the Pole, and even to have passed on the other side of it. They presume to doubt the existence of land on the north to Baffin's Bay, although Baffin was the best informed and most judicious seaman England could boast of; and they

**Alexander Pope: 'The Temple of Fame'*

even flatter themselves that commerce will be carried on in a direct route from London to Canton, by the pole, which makes a distance of only 2800 nautical leagues, whilst that by the Cape of Good Hope is 5500 leagues.

Two men, however, of great authority, do not participate in these exaggerated anticipations. Mr Scoresby, an experienced Greenland Captain, thinks that the polar seas are blockaded by ice, and proposes a journey to the pole by means of sledges drawn by reindeer. Captain Burney, who accompanied the immortal Cook, has published a pamphlet in which he proves clearly, that there exists a large extent of land to the north of Behring's Strait: he goes too far in supposing, that this land probably unites the continents of Asia and America: but it is very certain, that his arguments are sufficient to contradict the opinion of the existence of an open sea.

The gratitude which the English government merits from every friend to science, ought not to prevent us from examining upon what foundation their hopes of success in this enterprise rest. It is even an advantageous justice due to the commanders of the expedition, to point out to them, beforehand, the immense obstacles against which they have to contend.

Fixed and floating ices may be considered as the first of these difficulties. Admitting, for a moment, the non-existence of a polar continent – that Greenland, New Siberia, that the land to the north of Behring's Strait, and the land seen and coasted by Baffin, are, in reality, but four islands (as the maps of the 16th century appear to represent them); yet it is very probable, that the narrow seas which separate them are constantly choaked with ice. Captain Scoresby observed the ice form itself in the open sea, at more than twenty leagues from the coast of

Spitzbergen; and masses of ice arose from the bed of the sea. Thus, then, the principal argument in favour of an open sea is considerably weakened; it will be in vain for them to rely upon the removal of a barrier of ice, shaken by an earthquake, or broken by the strength of the currents... ...it is probable, that in the polar nights, that is to say, during our winter, the arctic seas are covered with ice. The history of different voyages furnish us with proofs of this.

The masses of floating ice arising from the water of the sea, and which is distinguished by its porous contexture (owing to the mixture of the volatile qualities of plants), sink four fifths of their thickness into the salt water, the latter being in a freezing state ... It appears certain, that the bays and straits of the Polar Seas (not generally very deep) are often obstructed by these masses resting at the bottom. The floating ice presents obstacles no less redoubtable. The concussion of these masses produces a tremendous noise, which warns the navigator with what facility his vessel would be dashed to pieces, if he were placed between two of these floating islands. It is even asserted, that the wood carried off by the currents, kindles by the violent collision caused by the motion of the ice; and flame and smoke arise amidst the gloom of eternal winter. Pieces of floating wood have often been found burnt at the extremities. In winter, the intense cold continually occasions these mountains of ice to split asunder, and at each moment, may be heard the explosion of these masses, which separate in enormous chasms. In all seasons the broken ice accumulates in the passages or gulfs, and opposes equally the attempts of individuals, who expose themselves on foot, and the progress of the vessel, whose motion becomes paralysed.

If to all these considerations be added, that the ordinary course of the ices from the Pole depends upon two constant and eternal causes, the seasons and the currents, the removal of the obstacles is only local and momentary; and it will be allowed that the Polar Seas will never afford a commercial route. Immense benefit may result to the fisheries from the discoveries which they hope to effect.

Conrad Malte-Brun

The fate of Sir John Franklin

Guardian, October 25 1854

Intelligence which may be fairly considered decisive has at last reached this country of the sad fate of Sir John Franklin and his brave companions. Dr Rae, whose previous exploits as an Arctic traveller have already so highly distinguished him, landed at Deal on Sunday, and immediately proceeded to the Admiralty, and laid before Sir James Graham the melancholy evidence on which his report is founded.

The following are extracts from Dr Rae's journal:

On the morning of the 20th we were met by a very intelligent Esquimaux, driving a dog sledge laden with musk ox beef. This man at once consented to accompany us two days' journey, and in a few minutes had deposited his load on the snow, and was ready to join us. Having explained to him my object, he said that the road by which he had come was the best for us, and, having lightened the men's sledges, we travelled with more facility. We were now joined by another of the natives, who had been absent seal hunting yesterday, but, being anxious to see us, had visited our snow-house early this morning, and then followed up our track. This man was very communicative, and on putting to him the usual questions as to his having seen 'white men' before, or any ships or boats, he replied in the negative; but said that a party of 'Kabloonans' had died of starvation a long distance to the west of where we then were, and beyond a large river. He stated that he did not know the exact place, that he never had been there, and that he could not accompany us so far. The substance of the information then and subsequently obtained from various sources was to the following effect:-

In the spring, four winters past (1850), while some Esquimaux families were killing seals near the north shore of a large island, named in Arrowsmith's charts King William's Land, about 40 white men were seen travelling in company southward over the ice, and dragging a boat and sledges with them. They were passing along the west shore of the above named island. None of the party could speak the Esquimaux language so well as to be understood, but by signs the natives were led to believe that the ship or ships had been crushed by ice, and that they were now going to where they expected to find deer to shoot. From the appearance of the men, all of whom, with the exception of an officer, were hauling on the drag ropes of the sledge, and looked thin, they were then supposed to be getting short of provisions, and they purchased a small seal, or piece of seal, from the natives. The officer was described as being a tall, stout, middle-aged man. When their day's journey terminated, they pitched tents to rest in.

At a later date the same season, but previous to the description of the ice, the corpses of some thirty persons and some graves were discovered on the continent, and five dead bodies on an island near it, about a long day's journey to the north-west of the mouth of a large stream, which can be no other than Back's Great Fish River (named by the Esquimaux Oot-koo-hi-ca-lik), as its description and that of the low shore in the neighbourhood of Point Ogle and Montreal Island agree exactly with that of Sir George Back. Some of the bodies were in a tent or tents; others were under the boat, which had been turned over to form a shelter; and some lay scattered about in different directions. Of those seen on the island it was supposed that one was that of an officer (chief), as he had a telescope strapped over his shoulders, and a double-barrelled gun lay underneath him.

From the mutilated state of many of the bodies and the contents of the kettles, it is evident that our wretched countrymen had been driven to the dread alternative of cannibalism as a means of sustaining life. A few of the unfortunate men must have survived until the arrival of the wildfowl (say until the end of May), as shots were heard and fresh bones and feathers of geese were noticed near the scene of the sad event.

There appears to have been an abundant store of ammunition, as the gunpowder was emptied by the natives in a heap on the ground out of the kegs or cases containing it, and a quantity of shot and ball was found below high-water mark, having probably been left on the ice close the beach before the spring commenced. There must have been a number of telescopes, guns (several of them double-barrelled), watches, compasses, &c. all of which seem to have been broken up, as I saw pieces of these different articles with the natives, and I purchased as many as possible, together with some silver spoons and forks, an order of merit, in the form of a star, and a small silver plate engraved 'Sir John Franklin, KCB.'

Dr Nansen's Farthest North

Guardian, February 15 1897

Being the Record of a Voyage of Exploration of the ship *Fram*, 1893-96, and of a Fifteen Months' Sleigh Journey by Dr Nansen and Lieutenant Johansen

On June 24 1893, Nansen set sail in his ship, the Fram, into the pack ice hoping that it might take him near the north pole as it passed by. In March 1895 Nansen, along with Hjalmer Johansen abandoned the ship and made a dash for the Pole

Nansen and Johansen set out on their long journey over the ice – how long it was to be none of them suspected. There were three sledges and 28 dogs. A complete list of the outfit occupies several pages and will well repay perusal, but we can only say here that the explorers did not take with them their thick fur clothing – the want of which they bitterly realised during the following winter – and did take with them a tent, of strong, undressed silk, which weighed only a fraction over three pounds, and proved the greatest comfort of their existence. The story of how these two human beings fought their way northwards is one of the most thrilling in the literature of travel, only exceeded in interest by the story of the still greater hardships and privations they had to endure after turning sourthwards before they reached land. It was April 8 that they reached their most northerly point. In his diary Nansen wrote:

'Ridge after ridge and nothing but rubble to travel over. We made a start at two o'clock or so this morning, and kept at it, but it grew too bad at last. I went on a good way ahead on snowshoes, but saw no reasonable prospect of advance, and from the highest hummocks only the same kind of ice was to be seen. It was a veritable chaos of ice blocks, stretching as far as the horizon. There is not much sense in keeping on longer; we are sacrificing valuable time and doing little. If there be much more such ice between here and Franz Josef Land, we shall indeed want all the time we have. I therefore determined to stop and shape our course for Cape Fligely.'

A 'banquet' celebrated the first appearance of man in historic times in such a latitude. It was at 86deg.13min. 6sec.N. that the return journey began, so that Dr Nansen and his companion had succeeded in getting nearly three degrees nearer to the northern axis of the earth than the holder of the previous highest record. A few days afterwards, after an especially long journey, Dr Nansen found to his dismay that their watches had run down, a misfortune which caused endless trouble and worry during their search for land to the southwards. They had hoped to reach Franz Josef Land in May, and so pass on to Spitzbergen in time to catch a whaler which would take them home that autumn. But day followed day, week followed week, and still there was nothing but the everlasting ice and snow, scored with great 'lanes,' caused by the action of the winds and currents on the immense floes. In some places they had no alternative but to wait until the movement of the ice made a passage practicable. At times progress seemed impossible. On some days after toiling for hours over rotten ice, lanes full of slush and brash, they found that they had actually drifted further north that when they had started on the day's march. Their dogs were ill-fed, and they themselves were on the shortest of short rations. One by one the dogs had to be killed to provide food for the survivors – a loathsome business from which both men shrank, but it had to be done. How they longed for open water, so that this endless dragging of sledges over the interminable ice might cease, and they could launch the light kayaks which now formed the most precious part of their equipment!

At length, on July 24, they sighted land, but it was a fortnight before they set foot on its inhospitable shores, though they deluded themselves with the hope that each day they must reach it. When at length the edge of the ice was reached and clear water lay in front of them it was August 6. Two days only remained, and these had to be sacrificed. The kayaks were launched, and the journey over the great drift ice was at an end. Where the travellers were they did not know, and it was not until next summer, when they had an opportunity of adjusting their observations, that they discovered that the islands they had struck lay to the east of the archipelago of Franz Josef Land. All hope of returning home that autumn had to be abandoned, and after alternate paddling and sledging they arrived, on August 26, at a spot on an island which Dr Nansen subsequently named 'Frederick Jackson Island.' Here they began to make preparations for passing the long dark Arctic winter.

Limits of space make it impossible for us even to indicate the conditions for their life for the next nine months. They succeeded with great difficulty in building a hut, partly of stones and partly excavated out of the ground; they shot bears and walruses for food, fuel, and light. It is on the record that they 'did not even have recourse to quarrelling to while away the time' – a test to which few men would care to submit. When the spring had come and the winter ice began to break up they set out once more, quitting their winter lair on May 19. Their dangers were not over yet. At one point their kayaks went adrift, and it was only by swimming in the ice-cold water that Nansen recovered the canoes, on which their one hope of safety rested. At another time a walrus attacked Nansen's fragile vessel.

In May 1896 they ran into a British expedition led by Frederick Jackson who helped them to safety. Meanwhile, the Fram broke free from the ice in August 1894 and sailed home to Norway.

Pioneering in Spitsbergen
Guardian, May 20 1897

There are not many parts of the earth left where the joys of exploration may still be tasted as fully as Sir Martin Conway and his half-dozen companions seem to have felt them in their recent trip to Spitsbergen – as we are desired to spell the name. The narrative of that expedition, which is now given to the world in a heavy, handsome volume, is full of references to this pleasure, which is worth earning at an expense from which the non-adventurous would shrink. Even that prosaic instrument the plane-table seems, as readers of his book on the Himalayas will have noticed, to have acquired a touch of romance in Sir Martin Conway's joyful though frigid hands. After pathetically explaining the manifold difficulties attendant on its use in a wet, windy and freezing country, he adds: –

Yet surveying a new land, with all its troubles, possesses great fascinations. It is delightful to behold the blank paper slowly covered with the semblance, however vague, of a portion of the earth's surface before unmapped. The interest of every view is increased when it has to be analysed structurally. Each mile traversed explains the mile that went before. Each corner turned reveals a tantalizing secret. Every march solves a problem, and leaves in the heart of the surveyor a delightful sense of something accomplished.

Elsewhere, whilst wandering with the plane-table in advance of his party, he breaks out into still stronger raptures:

'The scenery was, in fact, tame and dull, but circumstances invested it with a strange prestige. Its rich purple tones, its wide-expanding forms, its suggestive peeps of cloud-enveloped crags, sufficed to quicken the fancy, so that I walked along in the bleak dull days as in a dream, full of a nameless and indescribable delight.'

Here, perhaps, we behold chiefly the joy of being the first discoverer, almost the sole possessor, in search of which men go far afield, to the Caucasus and the Himalayas and New Zealand and the Andes, in quest of virgin peaks. But in many parts of Spitsbergen the scenery itself was the explorer's great reward. Sir Martin Conway is an adept in the art of word-painting, and can bring his impressions before the reader with all the skill for which one looks in a sometime professor of art. His Arctic experiences seem to have made him false even to his old alpine loves. 'Oh!' he cries:

'The glorious world, where man has no place and there is no sign of his handiwork, where Nature completes her own intentions unhindered and unhelped by him. Such pure snows no alpine height presents, nor such pale blue skies, nor that marvelous, remote, opalescent sea with its white flocks and its yet more distant shore. No alpine outlook penetrates through such atmosphere, so mellow, so rich. The Arctic glory is a thing apart, wilder, rarer, and no less superb than the glory of any other region of this beautiful world.'

The joy of discovery and the beauty of the scenery were certainly needed to recompense the party for the dangers and discomforts which they endured when 'blown by all the winds that pass, And wet with all the showers.' Sir Martin Conway writes cheerfully enough of these hardships, but they were evidently very considerable. Even he admits that he shuddered when he saw the naked crevassed face of a glacier which he had crossed with an unroped companion a few weeks before the snow had all melted from it, when they were under the happy impression that the numerous places where their ice axes would not touch bottom, really crevasses, were only deeper parts of the snow! Mr Garwood's little solitary adventure may be quoted as an instance of the risks which Arctic pioneers have to take.

The ice-foot at the Grit Ridge glacier reached to the junction of the two torrents, so that the second torrent, which was, in fact, the glacier stream, need not have been crossed at all. Its left bank, however, offered a more comfortable route, so we jumped across at a point where the overhanging ice-banks reached out towards one another. The torrent, with its floor and walls of purest ice, and its dark waters, was a beautiful thing. Garwood lingered behind to investigate the structure of the ice where at one point, its rod-like crystalline structure was displayed. He almost lost his life in consequence. The corniced bank gave way beneath his feet as he approached the edge to take a photograph. By a fortunate chance, he did not fall into the race of waters, whence he could not possibly have emerged alive, for the floor was ice, the torrent was in flood, and the walls overhung like a tunnel. He was facing the stream and he fell straight down; but his elbows behind his back caught on the newly broken edge, and there he hung suspended, unable to get any purchase with his feet, for they went right back against the slippery and still overhanging wall. He believes he remained in this dreadful position for 10 minutes before, by some twisting arrangement, he balanced himself on one hand and reached his geological hammer with the other. He ultimately dug this in, and made of it a prop by which he withdrew himself from a very nasty situation. Then he took the photograph and thereupon continued his way.

The weariness of perpetual tinned and condensed food and the difficulty of cooking in the tiny tents of the expedition intensified the hardships which the fearful nature of the boggy, slushy, stony country to be traversed already made bad enough. Sir Martin Conway dwells with gastronomic delight upon the occasional variations from chocolate tablets and Emergency Food. Here is an instance:

'I brewed a cup of tea – no brief task when the water has to be fetched from a snow-hole, into which it but slowly trickles, the lamp filled with spirit, cup cleaned, boiling water brought about with the normal denuberation of the watched pot, the compound strained, milk and sugar dislodged from their hiding places, and all by one pair of hands, within the confines of our shoulder-high tent. In half an hour the work was done. Then came the preparation of a mighty supper. In to the pot went the shredded fragments of two onions, a handful of dried vegetables, odds and ends of arrowroot and oatmeal, a lump of Bovril, a seasoning of Worcester sauce, and half a tin of Irish stew. Ye gods! What a jorum it was: and how it and the fried slices of rich plum pudding that followed suited the complaint of two hungry mortals whose food for many days had been stringy reindeer or concentrated rations.'

Some of the chief dangers of the expedition came from tourists brought out by the streams to Advent Bay, who had a curious delight in firing aimlessly right and left with the rifles which they had brought for the non-existent game. 'Many,' says Sir Martin Conway, 'were the narrow escapes of inoffensive onlookers. A bullet came closer over the tent of my companions.

Others whizzed near the heads of the salvage men working at the winter's wreck. One foolish creature is said to have mistaken a photographer with his head under a dark cloth for a reindeer, and put a cullet through his hat. Another, when we were away on the little steamer on the north coast, stalked and, I believe, fired upon our inoffensive ponies.'

The south pole: Amundsen's account of his journey

Guardian, March 11 1912

On February 10 1911, we began to work our way to the south. From this date until April 11 we established three depots, in which we stored a quantity of provisions. As there were no landmarks by which we could fix the depots, we identified them with flags which we placed seven kilometres on each side of them in an easterly and westerly direction …

Before the arrival of the winter we had 60,000 kilos of seal meat in our depot, which was enough for ourselves and the 110 dogs. We built eight dogs' houses, a combination of tents and snow huts. Having cared for our dogs we set about looking after ourselves. First we had to get light and air. The Lux lamp, which was 200 candle-power, gave us a brilliant light and kept up the temperature to 68 deg. F throughout the winter, while an excellent ventilation system gave us all the air we wanted. In direct communication with the hut, and dug out in the [ice] barrier, were the workshops, packing-rooms, cellars for provisions, coal, wood, oil, and a plain bath, a steam bath and observatories.

On October 20 the southern party started. We numbered five men, four sledges, and 52 dogs, and took with us provisions for four months. On the 23rd we made our depot at 80 deg., and went right ahead, in spite of dense fog. An error of two or three kilometres happened once in a while, but we were corrected by our depot flags and by these found our way without difficulty.

The journey from 82 deg. to 83 deg. became a pleasure trip. The ground was excellent, fine for sledging, and the temperature was all we desired. Everything went like a dance ...

On November 17, we arrived at the place where the land and [the Ross ice] barrier were connected. Here we made our head depot, taking provisions for 60 days on the sledges and leaving sufficient for 30 days there.

The land under which we lay, and which we now had to attack, looked quite imposing. The nearest summits along the barrier ranged from 2,000 feet to 10,000 feet in height, but several others further south were 15,000 feet or more. The next day we began the climb. The first part of it was an easy task, the ground rising in light slopes and well-filled mountain sides. It did not take a long time for our willing dogs to work their way up.

At a further point we met with some small but very steep glaciers. Here we had to harness 20 dogs to each sledge, and take the four sledges in two shifts. In some places the going was so steep that it was difficult to use our skis. Some big crevasses forced us from time to time to make a detour. The first day we climbed 2,000 ft.; the next day, during which the going was chiefly over small glaciers, we camped at a height of 4,500 ft. The third day we were obliged to go down on a very big glacier, the Axel Heibergs glacier, which divided the coast mountains and the mountains further south.

The next day began the longest part of our climb. Many detours had to be made in order to avoid the broad cracks and open crevasses. Our camp that night lay in very picturesque surroundings at a height of

5,000 ft. The glacier here was narrowed between the two 15,000 ft. mountains – Fridtjof Nansen and Don Pedro Christophersens mountains ...

We had now reached 5,600 ft., an almost incredible record, and it took us only four days from the barrier until we came up on the vast inland plateau. We camped that night at a height of 10,000 ft. Here we had to kill 24 of our brave dogs, and keep only 18, six for each of our three sledges. We stopped here for four days on account of bad weather.

On the 26th we encountered a furious blizzard. In the dense snowdrift absolutely nothing was to be seen, but we felt that, contrary to what we had anticipated, we were going downhill fast. The hypsometer, gave us that day a descent of 600ft. We continued our march the next day in a gale and a dense snowdrift. Our faces were badly frozen. We were in no danger, but we could see nothing. The weather cleared a little at dinner time, and revealed to our gaze a mighty mountain range to the east, and not far off.

On the 29th the weather calmed down, and the sun shone through. It was not the only pleasant surprise he gave us, for in our course stretched a big glacier running towards the south. At its eastern end was a mountain range going in a south-easterly direction. Over the western part of it no view was to be had, it being hidden in dense fog. At the foot of this glacier, the Devil's glacier, a depot for six days was established. It took us three days to surmount the Devil's glacier, the weather being extremely misty. On December 3 we gladly left this glacier, broken with numberless holes and crevasses.

The height, rising 9,100 ft, which lay before us looked in the mist and snowdrift like a frozen sea. It appeared to be a light, sloping ice plateau filled with small hummocks. The walk over this frozen sea was not pleasant. The ground under us was quite hollow, and it sounded as if we were walking on upturned empty barrels. One man fell through, then a couple of dogs. We could not use our skis on this polished ice. The sledges had the best of it. We named the place 'the devil's dancing room.' This part of our march was by far the most unpleasant.

On December 6 we attained our greatest height. According to the hypsometer and the aneroid we were 10,750ft. On December 8 we left the bad weather behind us. Before us lay an absolutely flat plateau, only here and there marked with a tiny sastrugi. In the afternoon we passed 88 deg 73 min, Shackleton's furthest point. In 88 deg. we camped and established our last depot, depot no.10 …

The day [December 14] went on without incident, and at 3pm we made a halt. According to our reckoning we had reached our destination. All of us gathered around the colours, a beautiful silken flag. All hands took hold of it, and, planting it on the spot, gave the vast plateau on which the pole is situated the name of the King Haakon VII Plateau. It was a vast plain, alike in all directions, mile after mile.

During the night we circled the camp in a radius of 18 kilometres. The following day in fine weather, we took a series of observations which lasted from 6am to 7pm. The result gave us 89 deg 55 min. In order to observe the position of the pole as close as possible we travelled as near true south as we could for the remaining nine kilometres.

On December 16 there we camped … There was a brilliant sun. Four of us took observations every hour of the day's 24. This much is certain; we observed the position of the pole as close as it is in human power to do so with the instruments we had – sextant and artificial horizon. The place circles in with a radius of eight kilometres.

On December 17, everything was in order on the spot. We fastened to the ground a little tent, which we had brought along, and fastened on top of it the Norwegian flag and the *Fram* pennant. The Norwegian home on the south pole was given the name Polheim.

The distance from our winter quarters to the pole was about 1,400 kilometres, so that on an average we had marched 25 kilometres a day. The weather proved favourable, and this made the journey home considerably easier than the march to the pole. We arrived at our winter quarters, which we had named Framheim, on January 25 1912, with two sledges and 11 dogs, and with all the party well. Our speed on the return journey averaged 36 kilometres a day.

Captain Scott's last journey

Guardian, February 11 1913

Captain RF Scott, the famous Antarctic explorer, and four other members of the British South Polar expedition have died amidst the southern ice. The five men were the whole southern party. They had reached the pole on January 18 1912, just over a month after Captain Amundsen, the Norwegian, and had struggled far back towards safety when they were overcome. Captain Scott and his last two companions died, it is believed, on March 29 1912. They had descended the glacier from the great inland plateau on which is the pole. From its foot they had marched northward to within a few miles of a stock of provisions at a place named by them One Ton Depot. There, almost in reach of succour, the struggle ended.

The Causes of disaster: Misfortunes on the way to the pole

Guardian, February 12 1913

Captain Scott, in the message written shortly before his death, set out summarily the main reasons for the disaster. They almost all relate to the earlier stages of the expedition … His reasons briefly are:-

(1) Loss of pony transport

'The loss of pony transport in March 1911 obliged me to start later than I had intended, and obliged the limits of stuff transported to be narrowed.'

Captain Scott started from New Zealand with 19 ponies, and lost nine for various reasons within four months … The use of ponies instead of dogs, it may be added, was the result of long and careful consideration by Captain Scott, but Amundsen has always thought that a mistake.

(2) Bad weather

'The weather througout the outward journey, and especially the long gale in 83 degrees south, stopped us … As we proceeded', says Captain Scott on December 10 1911, ' the weather grew worse, and snow-storms were frequent. The sky was continually overcast and land was very rarely visible. Under these circumstances it was most difficult to keep a straight course or maintain steady marches.'

(3) The Snow on the glacier

'The soft snow in the lower reaches of the glacier again reduced the pace. We fought these untoward events with a will and conquered, but it ate into our provision reserve … The men on foot sank to their knees, and the sledges to their crossbars continually… For four days we struggled through this morass, scarcely advancing five miles a day, although working ten to eleven hours. It was difficult to pitch camp or load sledges in such a surface.'

(4) Blizzards, cold weather and head winds on the return journey

'On our return journey we did not get a single completely fine day. This with a sick companion enormously increased our anxieties...Edgar Evans received a concussion to the brain. He died a natural death, but left us a shaken party.'

Terrible trials in the Antarctic

Guardian, May 4 1914

London, Sunday night: Dr Mawson, the famous Australian Antarctic explorer, arrived in London tonight from Paris. When the boat train reached Victoria station at seven o'clock, writes a London representative of the *Manchester Guardian*, there stepped out a man easily distinguished from his companions by his great height – slim with a keen face and a singularly pleasant smile. This was Dr Mawson, the man who came very near repeating the tragedy of Scott. He lived for twenty days on raw dog and snow, and reached his base half dead, only to see the ship that should have carried him to safety already out at sea.

Asked about the effects of his terrible experience on his health, Dr Mawson said that there had been no physical effects, but his nerves had suffered permanently. He held up his hand and remarked 'I can see the thumb trembling.' He had only two pounds of dogmeat left when he reached the depot, and if he had not struck the depot when he did he would never have reached his base. On this last journey he reached a treacherous slope of ice which he was only able to cross by making rough crampons for his feet out of a small aluminium theodolite which he had on the sledge. He spoke cheerfully of the extra year he had to spend in the Antarctic owing to missing the ship. It had enabled the party to do a good deal of valuable scientific work. During the three months of last year they were able, with the aid of the ship, to explore a long piece of the coast.

Dr Mawson was eloquent about the appalling weather in Adelie Land, a subject, he says, not hitherto sufficiently dealt with. The force and velocity of the winds was greater than could be imagined from the reports of blizzards brought back by Captain Scott's expedition. The average wind velocity for the whole year was 50 miles per hour. On one occasion a wind of 116 miles an hour was recorded, and it was frequently over 100 mph. A wind of 80 miles an hour would carry any buildings away. These tremendous winds were often accompanied with a temperature of minus 20. One newly-discovered effect of the tremendous winds in winter was the production of luminosity on objects, the result of the electricity caused by the wind blowing the snow particles together.

Asked as to the kind of minerals found, Dr Mawson said that it was shown that the coal formation which Shackleton and Scott reported in the Ross Sea area existed in King George the Fifth Land. Chunks of coal were brought up in dredging for deep-sea life. There was certainly a huge area of coal measures, but there was not much prospect at present of the coal being worked at a commercial profit. Among the many minerals of which evidence was found there may be some which will prove capable of commercial working.

Dr Mawson dwelt on the enormous value of the wireless communication which they were able to establish with the mainland through the intermediate station on Maquarrie Island. The fact that there were three

Antarctic bases thousands of miles apart working in unison by wireless made possible work in magnetism and meteorology otherwise out of the question. For instance, they had been enabled to fix the first absolute longitude for the Antarctic region.

'Oh, no,' Dr Mawson said, laughing. 'I don't think I shall go out again. I've just got married, as you may have seen in the papers, and a man isn't so venturesome when he's married. Besides, I hold that a man should not be over 30 for this kind of work. Between 25 and 30 a man is best able to stand the strain. How old am I? Thirty-one. Yes, too old at 30, if you like.'

Shackleton expedition: five months on the drifting ice

Guardian, June 2 1916

We print today Sir Ernest Shackleton's detailed account of his perilous adventures in the Antarctic which culminated in the loss of the *Endurance*, the landing of the whole expedition after severe privations on Elephant Island, and the daring and successful voyage in a small boat of Sir Ernest and five companions to South Georgia to seek help for the stranded members of the expedition.

'On December 6 1914, we left South Georgia; on the 8th we encountered heavy pack off the Sandwich group. The *Endurance* entered the pack and the vessel forced her way by a devious course for 1,000 miles through icebergs. The ice was becoming heavier and the floes were often 150 square miles in extent. We decided to land at the earliest opportunity and send the *Endurance* back to civilisation. We discovered a new land with 200 miles of coast line and great glaciers discharging into the sea. This we named Caird Coast.

A series of abnormal circumstances commenced. We observed a great migration of thousands of seals northwards, which was unaccountable at the time. We then experienced hard north-easterly gales, and sheltered behind large bergs amidst the surging sea. Eventually we found ourselves beset in the ice which never opened again. Summer conditions were non-existent. Contrary to all experience of the Antarctic in early February, the temperature was below zero. These conditions apparently accounted for the migration of the animal life.

In the middle of February there were signs of the ice opening, so, despite the shortage of coal, we attempted to break out. By the end of February there were 49 degrees of frost, and the old and the young packs were cemented together. It was impossible to land or extricate the ship, and so we prepared to winter. The winter was, generally speaking, mild, with the usual blizzards. The *Endurance* drifted south-west. We continued a zigzag drift across the Weddell Sea to the north-west, immovably fixed in the pack. In view of the possibility of pressure we placed our sledging stores on deck, and we trained the dogs for emergencies. Twenty dogs died from sickness. Some of the dogs disappeared on April 15 for 109 days …

In July the pressure became more intense, and there were ominous signs that the ship would be involved in the pressure. The ice rose into ridges of 40 feet in height, grinding into the floes ahead.

While examining the floes during a blizzard the ice split under my feet, and I had just rushed the dogs on board when with a grinding crash the pressure took us. The *Endurance* hove bodily out of the ice and was flung before the gale against masses of up-driven ice. The vessel stood the strain and by midday the pressure ceased. The ship keeled over half out of the water and with rudder split …

In the middle of October we broke clear of the floe, and a distant water-sky gave hope of ultimate safety. Then came renewed pressure, and the stern post was damaged. The ship was now leaking dangerously, and we put steam on the main engine, and all the pumps were continuously working.

On October 26 the floes commenced screwing and caused the ship's sides to open. We lowered the boats, sledges, and provisions on to the ice. On October 27 the end came. The terrific pressure culminated in tearing out the stern and rudder posts, the main deck breaking upwards. Icebergs pierced the ship; the water overmastered the pumps, extinguishing the fires. I ordered all hands on the ice. The pressure continuing near the ship we shifted the equipment.

At midnight a crack opened through the camp. The ship was submerged to the upper deck. Her fore and main mast had been twisted out by the pressure. The position of the party was serious. The nearest land and prospect of food was Paulet Island, 346 miles distant. We reorganised our equipment. All our scientific and film photographs were saved.

On October 30 we started relaying towards the north, seven dog teams relaying the provision sledges and the men hauling the boats in half-mile relays. Our advance was one mile in a day. New cracks and high pressure ridges impeded our progress, and the crossing of the open cracks was further endangered by the presence of killer whales, which would not hesitate to attack any man unfortunate enough to fall in.

After full consideration I decided, as it was impossible to move a large party across working ice, to camp in the vicinity of the wreck and our salved stores, and to depend on the northerly drift and the summer break-up. We salved stores from the ship by cutting through the ice and the main deck, and we grappled out a hundred cases of food. Our three boats – named respectively after donors to the expedition, the *James Caird*, *Dudley Docker*, and *Stancombe-Wills* – were prepared for a sea journey. For the next two months we drifted north. The *Endurance* sank on November 20.

On December 23 we left Ocean camp, as the ice appeared close enough to travel over. Hauling the boats, marching night and day through deep snow, and cutting pressure ridges, the whole party, with two boats advanced nine miles in five days.

On December 28 rotten ice made it impossible to proceed, the boats sinking through the brash. We were forced to retreat and set up 'Patience Camp.' There were passed January, February, and March, 1916, slowly drifting north. The floe ice grew small under the attack of neighbouring icebergs and gales, and was finally reduced to 100 yards square. In January we shot five of our dog-teams owing to the shortage of food. The party was put on stringent rations because of the dearth of seals and the limited hunting radius.

By the middle of March the winter commenced, with low temperatures, long nights, and heavy blizzards. We were drifting north rapidly, and a northerly swell indicated that open water was close. On April 7 we sighted Clarence Island (the most easterly of the South Shetlands). Here the party had a narrow escape. A great berg driving through the pack missed us by only 200 yards. On April 8 the floe on which our camp was pitched split to pieces under the influence of the swell. As the ice opened we launched the boats. The tide rip driving the ice almost finished our expedition. Rowing through masses of pack, we made northward and pulled the boats up on a floe for the night.

A heavy swell set in at midnight, and the floe split under the tent. We pulled one man out of the water before the floes closed together. On the 10th we made westward in a heavy snow squall and reached open sea, but there we met a high swell which forced us to retreat to the pack ice. The sea was too heavy for our deeply laden open boats, so during the night I drastically reduced the equipment, and we camped on a floe-berg. At noon on the 11th our opportunity came. The ice opened suddenly, and we flung the boats into the sea over the icefoot of reeling berg.

We proceeded westward all night, and rowed throughout the 12th, continuing west. That night no camping place was found, and we fastened the boats to the lee side of a floe-berg in a heavy swell. The wind, suddenly shifting, drove the boats against the berg. We cut the painters and escaped to the open sea. The sea surface was freezing and the temperature stood at zero. Several of the party were suffering from exposure.

On April 14 we sighted Elephand Island 40 miles away. On the morning of the 15th we reached the north end of the island. There were inaccessible cliffs, but it was decided to attempt to land on a small beach in view of the condition of the party, which had now been without water or hot food for two days. All the equipment was sodden. On landing we found that several members of the party were on the verge of physical and mental collapse. An inspection of the beach showed that it was impossible to remain, as it was covered at high spring tides. On the 16th I sent Wild to search the coast for a safer landing. On the 17th we proceeded westward, but were nearly blown to sea owing to strong winds and weakness of a large number of the party. We landed again through a heavy surf. We found that the beach would be untenable in heavy gales, but proceeded to cut a hole in the ice slope, above reach of the waves.

Owing to the seriousness of the situation, and the shortage of food, and the inadequate protection against winter I decided to make an endeavour to reach South Georgia, 750 miles distant, to obtain help, leaving the main party on Elephant Island in charge of Frank Wild, whose judgment, ability, and experience were a valuable asset to the expedition. Our largest boat, the *James Caird*, 22 feet long, was covered by the carpenter with sledge runners, box-lids and canvas.

On April 24 I set out with volunteers – namely, Worsley, Crean, MacNish, Macarthy, and Vincent. We passed through the stream ice and ran north with a fair wind during the first night. Day after day we made progress towards the goal, but the sub-Antarctic ocean maintained its evil winter reputation. Snowstorms and gales swept over us for the next fortnight, and only three times did we get sight of the sun for observation

On the sixth day we were forced to jettison oars and other equipment to relieve the top weight owing to the boat being heavily iced up. All our equipment and sleeping gear was soaked through. We were constantly at work breaking the ice off the sides and rudder, baling water, and scraping ice out of the boat day and night. All the crew became superficially frostbitten.

On the 14th day we sighted the cliffs and the west coast of South Georgia during a clearance in a snowstorm, and we stood in for the land, but, observing seas spouting on uncharted reefs, we hauled off for the night. On May 9 the wind again increased to a hurricane, and enormous seas were running on a dead lee shore. We saw nothing till the afternoon, when between squalls we found we were drifting on to the cliffs. One chance remained. We set a reefed sail. The boat stood the strain and was kept afloat by continuous baling. The wind shifted at the very crisis, enabling us to clear the land.

I decided in view of the condition of the party and the shortage of water, to beach the boat and try to cross the island to the whaling station on the east coast. On May 19 I started across the island. As Vincent and McNish were unfit to march, I took Crean and Worsey with me. As the interior of the island was quite unknown, I took three days' provisions and cooking stove, but no other equipment. Thirty-six hours continuous marching covered 30 miles over glaciers, across mountain ridges, and snowfields from 2,000 ft to 4,000 ft above sea level. We made good progress, assisted by the moonlight. We reached Stromness whaling station in the afternoon of May 20. This is the first time the island of South Georgia has been crossed.

I received every assistance from the manager of the whaling station, Mr Sorllee, who despatched a whaler the same night to bring round the remainder of the party.'

The Italia Adventure

Guardian, July 29 1930

With the Italia to the North Pole, by Umberto Nobile (Allen and Unwin 15s)

Most newspaper readers will still remember the excitement at the end of May 1929, when it was announced that the dirigible *Italia*, having successfully flown over the north pole, was missing and the frantic international search for it in which Amundsen lost his life, and remember also the sad controversy that arose on the reason for the disaster and the leader's actions. This is Nobile's answer to his critics – including his official ones – but it is not polemical. It is far more the record of exciting adventure that ended in tragedy and did not prove that the dirigible was the ideal medium for Arctic exploration. There is at least no particular vindication of its scientific importance, and it remains rather a story of personal experience, plain in form but coloured by southern warmth of feeling.

Much of the record is already known in one form or another. Here it is put in order, and returns one the authentic thrill of the continuous story – the bustle of preparations, the emotional flag-dropping on the Pole, the fierce duel with the wind, the loss of direction, and the smash on 'a formless contorted jumble of pointed ice peaks stretching to the horizon.' It is here that the real story begins. The smash of May 25 was catastrophic. Six of the crew were missing, one was dead, three were injured: the leader had his right arm and leg broken. The nine survivors built a rough tent and waited. Perhaps an English writer would hardly have been so frank, but Nobile justifies the title of the next section, 'Souls laid bare.' Death by cold or starvation stared them in the face, and in its grim presence men were revealed for what they were. Some could not move. Others were all for making the attempt to get away. Lack of food made a move imperative; the lucky shooting of a bear with a Colt eased the food crisis, but did not abate the eagerness of those who wanted to go, not trusting that the world would hear that SOS call launched every two hours. On May 30, after argument at times heroic, at times rather ridiculous, three men went off. The six in the red tent went on unbaring their souls till June 6, when their wireless told them their message had been picked up, and finally next day the Italian *Citta di Milano* spoke to them – 'an hour of indescribable joy.'

Then came the anxiety of the waiting – equally an unbaring – period, with the need for shifting camp and fears that the wireless would break down. On June 20 *Maddelena* flew over the camp and dropped provisions, and finally, on June 25, Lundberg landed at their camp. The main criticism of Nobile is that he allowed himself to be rescued first and left his comrades. There seems no reason why Nobile should not have gone first: he could do no good by staying – he was helpless from his injuries – nor could priority of rescue have any more sentimental advantage to any of the others. It had been agreed by the six that he should go first, and Lundborg also insisted that he should, as his advice and knowledge were needed at the rescue base. So he went, and the world, or most of it, said he had deserted his men.

The attack on Nobile came from Italy in its fiercest onset, for what reasons we are not told. The attack had its superficial justification and its easy analogy of the captain on the sinking ship. But the analogy is not perfect. Nobile himself had to decide what was his duty. Others might have decided differently, but no one can say after reading his own story that any unworthy motive entered into the decision. There is in this narrative plenty of material for criticism. There were faults of organisation, leadership, judgment; but whatever may be said of these on the main issue – the 'desertion' – he did what he did because he felt there was no moral obligation to the reverse.

Arctic mystery solved

Guardian, August 23 1930

A 30 years' mystery of the Arctic has been solved by the finding on White Island, between Spitzbergen and Franz Josef Land, of the body of the Swedish explorer and balloonist Salomon August Andrée by a Norwegian scientific expedition carrying out research work in the Arctic under the leadership of the geologist Dr Horn. A second body was also found in the remains of the camp which the flyers had made. Both bodies were in a good state of preservation.

The discovery reveals what must have been one of the grimmest fights for life ever made by human beings trapped in the polar wastes. Andrée took off in a balloon from Danes Island, Spitzbergen, with two companions in July 1897, intending to drift with the prevailing air current over the north pole to America. Andrée, who was born on 1854, became an engineer, and was examiner to the Patents Office. He had one ruling passion, ballooning, and his confidence in his theories led him to attempt his hazardous flight. When no further news of him and his companion was heard several expeditions were sent in search, and for years there were periodical rumours that the balloon had been found in Siberia or messages washed ashore on northern coasts. Hope that the men might have survived for some time was strengthened by the fact that Andrée's drag-rope consisted in part of a succession of canisters containing food.

The discovery of the lost flyers' camp was made by the Norwegian expedition on August 6, on the south-west side of White Island. The camp was situated about 150 yards from the shore, and bore many evidences that the explorers had lived there for some time after disaster overtook them. A boat and a sledge, a book of observations, and equipment marked 'Andrée's Polar Expedition, 1896,' were among the objects found.

The body of the explorer, fully dressed, was found only a few yards from the boat. The remains were imprisoned in a thin glassy coating of ice. In Andrée's pockets were his dial-altimeter and various other items. Quite near him lay another body, also well preserved, which has not yet been identified. In the boat were vestiges of what were apparently human remains. The camp had been visited by bears but had been little disturbed.

Antarctic between the lines

Observer, October 26 1958

The Crossing of Antarctica, by Sir Vivian Fuchs and Sir Edmund Hillary (Castell, 30s.); *The White Desert*, by Noel Barber (Hodder & Stoughton, 16s.)

Sir Ernest Shackleton, perhaps the greatest polar explorer of all, first conceived and attempted the crossing of the Antarctic continent, 'the last great polar journey that can be made.' Forty-five years later Sir Vivian Fuchs and his party attempted and achieved this journey of 2,158 miles across the icy desert. The journey was carried out in the modern manner with vehicles and planes and an elaborate scientific programme, but it was conceived and executed in the spirit – half spiritual, half adventurous – of the dreamer; the spirit of Scott and Amundsen and Lawrence of Arabia. Unfortunately it has had, as yet, no chronicler to make it live. Every schoolboy has been brought up on *Scott's Last Expedition* and *The*

Seven Pillars of Wisdom but few schoolboys of the future will be brought up on *The Crossing Of Antarctica.*

The advertisements describe the book as 'beautiful and dramatic.' Beautiful it is, for all the photographs are good, many magnificent, and the colour plates are almost unbelievable. They show some of the pure colouring – pale and delicate greens, blues and pinks mingling without any discernible boundary into each other – that is found only in polar regions. It is, however, one of the limitations of photography that it cannot give any feeling of cold or of time. It is all too easy to gain the impression that the Antarctic is the world's most beautiful continent and forget the long days of blizzard and searing wind.

But dramatic the book is not. It is a disappointing, flat record of a journey which demanded the utmost skill, patience and perseverance. One gets no glimpse of the characters of the party through the tangle of incident, topographic detail (the maps are appalling) and records of place and time and weather. The determination in Fuchs's character emerges only between the lines, and the feelings – the hopes and fears – of the party not at all. Tension appears only in the accounts of the two journeys from Shackleton to South Ice through areas of enormous crevasses, and then only when Fuchs turns to his diary:

'As the vehicles continued to move slowly, I saw a cloud of snow rising in the air from an immense crater which had appeared only six feet to the left of the Weasel... with dark and deep caverns descending to unknown depths ... the whole thing appeared as though a bomb had fallen. The hole was large enough to have swallowed Sno-cat, Weasel, sledge and all, but by amazing good fortune the bridge broke to the left of the vehicles and not under them!'

Amundsen crossing the Antarctic

And how dramatic is this to someone who has never peered into the hungry, lifeless blue jaws of a crevasse?

To appreciate Fuchs's qualities – and the very different restless character of Sir Edmund Hillary – one must read Noel Barber's *The White Desert.* Barber was the only Englishman to be present as an outsider at the great climaxes of the story; the arrival at the Pole and the ending at Scott Base. He has written a workmanlike, readable account of the expedition and also told us something of the routine and feelings of a journalist on such an unusual assignment: the excitement, the boredom ('I went, as usual, to the camp cinema for my nightly hour or so of stale romance'), the constant battle to keep open his lines of communication.

There is exaggeration, notably in describing Hillary's journey to the pole as a 'race,' and there is one strange omission. Throughout, Barber refers to the differences of opinion between Fuchs and Hillary which caused so much controversy midway through the expedition. Yet when he comes to the point he, the only outsider who could, does not tell the story but only remarks, 'What is now spoken of as a disagreement was much more than that.'

It is left to Fuchs himself to tell the story, quoting in full the messages which passed between Hillary and himself. And indeed it was a much overplayed story for which the expedition itself must partly be blamed. When one newspaper has exclusive rights on a story of national importance others will do everything to grasp at the trickles of news which seep out. But then Britain, unlike the Americans and Russians, always leaves enterprises of this kind, as Noel Barber says, to 'the Byrons fighting for a good cause, lost or otherwise'. And Fuchs, like Scott and Shackleton before him, had always to fight under the crippling burden of raising money from the public and industry.

Both books, particularly Barber's, which was published two months earlier, suffer from having had to be written quickly. This is a pity, for there is a lasting quality about the enterprise which is lacking in these books.

Christopher Brasher

Dismantling a national monument

Guardian, November 29 1979

Scott and Amundsen by Roland Huntford (Hodder, £13.95)

Mr Huntford's enormous work is a demolition act, to be parked alongside Richard Aldington's attack on Lawrence of Arabia, which it resembles – in the thoroughness of its research and the effective way this is organised. By treating in one volume the lives of the winner and the loser in that race for the south pole, he challenges every Englishman to get Scott into perspective instead of genuflecting mindlessly before a national monument.

His great achievement here is to write a life of Amundsen such as we have not had before: an expert in Norwegian affairs and a fluent speaker of the language, he has tapped many documents (including the explorer's polar diary) which had previously been ignored. And there is is no doubt at all that Scott comes badly out of a comparison between the two as expedition leaders. Where Amundsen was careful, far-sighted, tough-minded, adaptable, ready to learn from earlier mistakes, Scott was negligent, myopic, vacillating , rigid, and plain stupid. That the Norwegians generally enjoyed better weather that the Englishmen was partly a matter of luck. That Amundsen's men and dogs actually put on weight as they romped home from the pole, while Scott's party slowly starved to death hauling their own sledges, was the result of intelligent planning on one side and shocking mismanagement on the other.

Yet this book is seriously flawed by its author's own cast of mind. He is perfectly balanced about Amundsen, giving due weight to strengths and weaknesses. He is totally cynical about Scott, finding it hard to say anything in his favour, quite willing to have it all ways in his eagerness to nail the man. One minute Scott is berated for mawkish sentimentatality towards dogs, the next we are told that he found them distasteful, a contradiction that Mr Huntford may not have noticed in his passionate antipathy.

We are also told, so many times I lost count, that good luck goes to those who deserve it, or variations thereon: which is tripe. And, gradually, it seems that Mr Huntford is bent on putting down not just Scott but as much of the British countenance as he can manage to indict in one volume. If there is one sentence which sums up his tone when he turns from the Norwegians to the British it is this: 'Straining as if each mile was his last, Scott provided the heroic self-punishment so dear to the heart of the British public of whom he was never aware.'

I don't in the least mind the dismantling of a national monument, and I can put up with some sharp home truths about the nation at large. But I think it's a shame that what might have been the definitive study of two brave men and their companions has become lopsided through prejudice and cheapened by sneers. By the end I was fairly clear about the nature of Captain Scott's problems, but I was left to speculate wildly about Mr Huntford's.

Geoffrey Moorhouse

The perils of snow business

Guardian, August 30 1993

'Polar exploration,' remarked Apsley Cherry-Garrard, a member of Scott's 1914 Antarctic expedition and author of *The Worst Journey In The World*, 'is at once the cleanest and most isolated way of having a bad time ever devised.' Eighty years later Sir Ranulph Fiennes and Dr Mike Stroud are reinforcing this notion with their public comments on each other's behaviour during their frostbitten trudge earlier this year across Antarctica. When their separate accounts are published in the coming weeks, the public will learn even more about what happens when stiff upper lips tremble and crevasses appear in the traditional reticence of chaps who trek into the unknown for queen and country (and glory and loot).

Two chapter headings of Stroud's book tell us what to expect: 'A Question Of Leadership' and 'Also Ran'. The first reveals a squabble over who was the leader of the two-man expedition, the Great Explorer or the sturdy MoD nutritionist. Fiennes has already delivered pre-emptive strikes at the implications of 'Also Ran', giving his partner the small-black-dot-in-the-distance treatment in newspaper extracts from his book and off-the-cuff remarks. Fiennes's anecdotes unfailingly put the physically smaller (but, friends say, intellectually superior) Stroud trailing behind.

Stroud will counter in his book, *Shadows On The Wasteland* (which originally had the ambiguous title of *Poles Apart*), by describing in tactlessly compassionate detail his partner's insecurity about his age (49 – Stroud is 37) and his difficulty in managing the 485lb sledge load. (In 1903 Scott hauled loads of only 175lb.) Stroud claims he even offered to take some of Fiennes's burden. Vexing stuff for Ranulph Twistleton-Wykeham Fiennes, a man who has led British expeditions since the Jostedalsbre glacier adventure of 1970.

But what has happened to the Oates spirit? Where is the stony discretion of a Scott, who preferred death to failure, or even the pragmatic tact of a Shackleton, who preferred failure to death?

Now there is a new twist. Friends say the two men are telephoning each other three times a week, their friendship repaired (they have been on three expeditions together). So what will happen when the books, deep-frozen parcels of antagonism and rivalry, are distributed by their publishers from next month? There has been a tactical adjustment already. At Jonathan Cape, Stroud's publisher, they say that while originally the two men were going to appear side by side in television and radio interviews, now their publishers prefer not. 'Because of the kind of questions that might come up,' nudge-nudged a spokesperson for Cape. The two heroes now find themselves trapped inextricably in a crevasse more pitiless than anything the polar regions could put in their way: commercial publishing imperatives.

There may have been a time when brave, if slightly daft, men were driven only by personal obsession to explore nature's dark or blinding wastes; now they offer themselves to sensory deprivation on the say-so of commercial backers who in effect choose the spot. Sir Ranulph hates the polar regions; he sees himself as a desert man. But there is no money nowadays in sand, only in snow.

It is not surprising that Fiennes and Stroud became irritated with each other as they stomped across the most barren and featureless territory on earth. Unlike the scientific polar expeditions, which drift along coastal areas by the most fertile seas in the world, these men did not have an opportunity to pass the time of day with a penguin or exchange barking civilities with a seal. Unlike Scott, they did not come across helpful depots of stores laid along the route; Fiennes and Stroud were on an 'unaided' expedition. Scott had ponies, four companions and even motor vehicles. It was indeed an affair of *Mind Over Matter*, as Fiennes calls his book.

Fiennes and Stroud tottered, mostly in silence, across a 1,350-mile plateau, hating each other; it was white on the ground, mostly white in the sky and with not as much as an outcrop of rock to vary the landscape. 'It was he now who was finding the pulling harder,' writes Stroud. 'He felt it sorely. During 30 years of expeditioning, his phenomenal physical strength … had never been challenged. Now, although only marginally slower, he had to accept the effects of his age and suffered inner torment as he tried to come to terms with it.' Stroud offered to take some of his load: 'It would slow me up, make you faster.'

Fiennes confessed his hatred of Stroud. 'Don't worry,' said the benign nutritionist, 'I more than hated you in the Arctic (a previous expedition).'

Ed Douglas of *Mountain Review* said that such antagonism was normal: 'In such conditions a natural antipathy builds up. You are hitting your reserves of physical energy all the time coming up against barriers of your own self and trying to beat these barriers. When two very competitive men are involved, rivalry is inevitable. In old Himalayan expeditions, when only two or three could get to the top there was fantastic rivalry. This is a game in which you could lose digits, fingers, toes. Resentment and rivalry can be expected.'

Publishing strategies and the more than £1million raised by Fiennes and Stroud for multiple sclerosis apart, is there another more profound force at work behind these punishing expeditions? Twenty years ago in *The Ulysses Factor*, JRL Anderson analysed the explorers' motives and found them bound to the aspirations and fears of the tribe/countries in which they lived. 'The Ulysses factor (named after the hero of the Odyssey) in man,' Anderson wrote, 'being genetically a survival factor, has naturally emerged in forms contributing to the survival or increased prosperity of the clan ... Over the centuries of European expansion the most successful nations were those in which the Ulysses factor in individuals was most active, the Norse, the Portuguese, the Spaniards, the English.'

But a diminished great power has equal need of a Ulysses figure. 'It is,' Anderson wrote, 'as if the instinct for national survival in nations whose material power has diminished, or which are too small for the exercise of great power in modern terms, is expressing itself through individuals, substituting the conquest of Annapurna or Everest for imperial glory.'

Friends say they would not be surprised if Fiennes and Stroud set off together again fairly soon, if only to come to the aid of a nation almost as battered as they are.

Peter Lennon

Obituary: Sir Wally Herbert

Guardian, 15 June 2007

Sir Wally Herbert, who has died aged 72, was one of the last explorers of the polar regions who was able to make major contributions to geographical discovery and research. From a family background of travel, and an early education in Africa, he spent time travelling throughout the Americas and Europe. His passion for polar regions began in the Antarctic and later extended to the Arctic, where he made the first crossing of the frozen ocean. As time went on, he made a gentle transition to become a writer and artist of the scenes he knew so well.

Wally was born in England into an army family, and went with his family to Egypt aged three, and then to South Africa for nine years. After finishing school, he joined the army, where he studied at the Royal School of Military Survey. Subsequently, he spent 18 months surveying in Egypt and Cyprus. From there he began a slow journey back to Britain through Turkey and Greece, drawing portraits for his board and lodging.

In 1955, he obtained a post in the Antarctic with the Falkland Islands Dependencies Survey (which became the British Antarctic Survey in

1961). He was based at Hope Bay station, near the northern end of the Antarctic peninsula, where much of his work involved surveying which included glaciological studies. Field work was an essential component of this and most of his extensive traverses were made by dog sled; he became an expert in the care and running of husky dogs.

His longest journey was along the mountainous spine of the Antarctic peninsula from Hope Bay (62o23S) to Portal Point (64o33S). This included transits of the notoriously narrow Catwalk and the Waist, where the Herbert Plateau narrows abruptly. During these two years, he sledged some 5,000km. This was when, as with several of his contemporaries, he developed a persistent passion for the polar regions. Wally's experience with dog sledding led him to a job with the New Zealand Antarctic programme, where his first commission was to go to the west coast of Greenland to purchase dogs for the Antarctic. During this time, he learned much of the Inuit methods of dog driving and developed an enduring interest in their way of life. He continued to the Antarctic to join the New Zealanders with his selected team of 13 dogs.

As leader of the 1961-2 southern exploration party, he surveyed a large area of the Queen Maud range, where he ascended the route up the Beardmore glacier, discovered by Ernest Shackleton in 1908 and followed by Captain Scott in 1911. A request to continue to the south pole was not sanctioned, so his programme was exploration of new territory southwards along the Transantarctic mountains. At the head of the Axel Heiberg Glacier, his party ascended Mount Nansen and descended by a similar route to that taken by Roald Amundsen in 1911, during which he found one of Amundsen's survey cairns. This was the first retracing of these historical traverses accomplished during the heroic age of exploration. Wally returned to Britain in 1962 and wrote his first book about his experiences, *A World of Men.*

In 1963, he conceived an idea for a major Arctic expedition and began careful planning, including living with the Inuit in the far north west. The following spring, he set out with three dog teams and four Inuit to trace the routes described by Otto Sverdrup (1898-1902) and Frederick Cook (1908-09). This led from Greenland to Ellesmere Island and proved a difficult test, largely across pack-ice, for men and equipment.

Wally's best known polar journey was as leader of the British trans-Arctic expedition (1968-9), with Allan Gill, Roy Koerner and Kenneth Hedges. Their equipment included four sleds and 40 dogs. The journey began from a base at Point Barrow, Alaska, where the first difficulty to be overcome was access from the shore to the constantly drifting Arctic ice fields. It was planned to make the traverse in three travelling periods, interrupted by the Arctic winter and the summer melt period, when travel over the pack becomes impossible.

After crossing some 1,900km of rough drifting ice, they established a summer camp, in July 1968, at 81deg 22N 165deg 29W, which became known as 'Meltville'. Unfortunately, they were not able to reach a position where the drift of the trans-Arctic ice-stream was in their favour (they were drifting around the north pole rather than towards it). This necessitated the expedition camping there for the winter, during which they continued to drift anti-clockwise but not much closer to the pole.

After midwinter, the floe on which they had camped broke in two and, in February, shattered. However, they had to remain until the sunlight returned before continuing the journey which passed the northern pole of inaccessibility. The geographic north pole was attained on

April 6 1969. Wally and the other three were unquestionably the first men to have reached this point over the ice surface. From the pole, over difficult ice, they continued to Vesle Tavloya, the most northerly island of the Svalbard archipelago, which was reached on May 29 1969, 464 days from Point Barrow. Other than receiving air-drops, contact with the rest of the world was by radio only.

For this achievement, the first surface traverse of the Arctic, the longest traverse across the Arctic Ocean, reaching the northern pole of inaccessibility and north geographic pole, 6,700km over the pack-ice, Wally was awarded an Arctic bar to his Polar medal and received awards from the Royal Geographical Society and other institutions. His book of the expedition, *Across the Top of the World*, was published in 1969. Shortly after his return, he married Marie McGaughey, and within two years they lived, with their baby daughter, Kari, on an island off north-west Greenland making a film about the Inuit hunters.

Greenland was again Wally's polar base when, between 1977 and 1979, he, with Allan Gill, attempted to circumnavigate the island by dog sled and umiak (traditional boat), beginning and ending at Thule. It was estimated that the journey would take 16 months and cover 13,000km. Difficult ice and weather conditions, however, made it impossible. On midsummer day in 1978, they were near Loch Fyne (East Greenland); Wally wrote: 'We were forced to take to the land and haul the sledges across steaming tundra and rock bare of snow, swollen rivers, baked mud flats, sand-dunes, swamps and stagnant pools. We were blasted by dust-storms and eaten alive by mosquitoes.' Mesters Vig was ultimately reached, but the circumnavigation was abandoned, and has yet to be accomplished. Subsequently, he led filming expeditions to north-west

Greenland, Ellesmere Island and the north pole for a second time (but by aircraft).

From this period, Wally's literary and artistic career began to dominate. He also lectured extensively. He made a specialised study of the north pole controversy (the problems of Frederick Cook in 1908 and Robert Peary in 1909), and although his analysis effectively resolved rival claims, *The Noose of Laurels* (1989) was not able to quench many of the passionate opinions. He also worked on his autobiography, *The Third Pole*, and on a book of his paintings, *The Polar World* (2007). He was knighted in 2000.

Wally is commemorated in the Antarctic by names of a mountain range and a plateau, and, in the Arctic , the most northern mountain of Svalbard also bears his name.

Walter William Herbert, explorer, born October 24 1934; died June 12 2007

Bob Headland

TWO

DESERTS

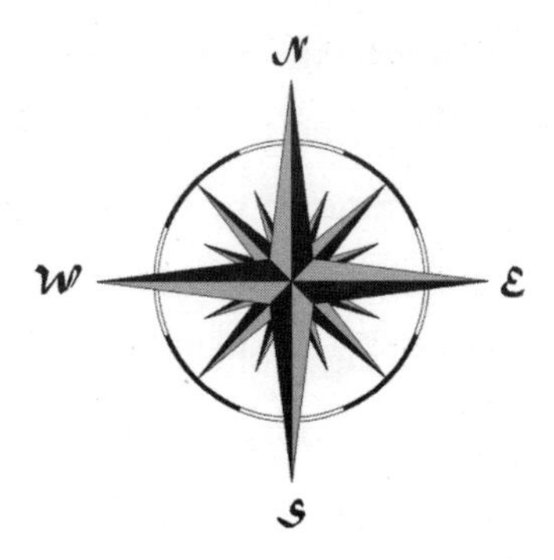

The murder of Major Gordon Laing

Guardian, August 2 1828

Major Laing arrived at Tripoli in May, 1825, with the view of proceeding from thence through the desert to Timbuctoo, and then following the course of the Niger to its termination. He left Tripoli on the July 17, in the company of Sheik Badani, a highly respectable man, who had resided 22 years in Timbuctoo, and who promised to conduct Major Laing to that city in two months and a half, and to deliver him over to the great Marahout Mooktar, by whose influence he would be able to proceed farther in any direction that might be required.

His journey commenced under unfavourable circumstances; owing to the petty wars which so often trouble these countries, he could not pass the Gharian mountains, and was forced to make a circuit of 1,000 miles to reach Ghadamis, which is no more than 250 from Tripoli. In the course of this journey, all his instruments were destroyed by the heat of the weather or the jolting of the camels. His barometers were broken; his hygrometers rendered useless by the evaporation of the ether; the tubes of his barometers snapped by the warping of the ivory; the glass of the artificial horizon was so dimmed by the friction of the sand, which insinuated itself everywhere, as to render an observation very difficult; his chronometer stopped, owing probably to the same cause; and, to wind up the catalogue of his misfortunes, the stock of his rifle was broken by the foot of a great gouty camel treading upon it.

At Ghadamis, of which his friend Babani was governor, he was well treated, being lodged in a house with a large garden, and fed at the governor's expense. It contains six or seven thousand inhabitants, and is a place of considerable trade. The Kofilas or caravans to and from Sudan pass through it, and a tax is paid to the roaming tribe of the Tuaric for the privilege of crossing the desert without being subject to plunder. The town, which is four or five miles in circumference, including its gardens, is surrounded by a low mud wall, and has in its centre a pool of water, out of which all the streets and gardens receive a plentiful supply.

On December 3 1825, he reached Ensala, about 500 miles south-west from Guadamis in the desert belonging to the Tuaric. On approaching the town, some thousands of all ages and both sexes came out to meet the Christian traveller. Nothing could excel the kindness and hospitality of these people, which our traveller returned by listening to their complaints and administering medicines to the best of his ability. The kofila left Ensala on January 10, and, after travelling about 220 miles right south, entered the desert Tenezarof, a mere waste of sand, destitute of all verdure, and as flat as a bowling-green. He was now about twenty journeys or 300 miles from Timbuctoo, and stated in a letter that he was in good health and spirits. Shortly after this letter was received, reports reached Tripoli of the kofila having been attacked by robbers, of Laing's servant, with several others, being killed, and himself wounded. It was added, that he had effected his escape to Marabout Mooktar, who usually resides at a spot five days journey by the Maherrie (or fleet camel) from Timbuctoo. After a long interval, a letter was was received at Tripoli on September 26, which tended to confirm these reports. It was addressed to his wife, the daughter of the British consul, whom he had married just previous to setting out. It mentioned that he had been indisposed but had recovered, and expected in less than 20 days to be in Timbuctoo, from which he intended to make his way to the coast; that he had been much annoyed by the tuaric, and had a severe cut in his fore finger.

About the middle of October further accounts were received, reporting that he was safe with Mooktar at his residence not far from Timbuctoo, and repeating the story of the attack by the tuaric. At length his Arab servant Hamet arrived at Tripoli, with two letters written by himself, dated July 1 and 10 1826, from which, and the servant's verbal statement, the fact of his being assailed and maltreated by robbers was too clearly established. It appears that while the kotila, which consisted of 45 persons, was on its march through the desert, and about 11 days south of Tuat, it was joined by 20 tuaric mounted on Maherries. Five days after the tuaric joined him, they fell suddenly on the party, 'leaving Raboni and his people unmolested', but attacking the others with guns, spears, swords, and pistols. They surrounded Laing's tent, fired at him while in bed, and cut him so severely in the thighs and arms, that he was left behind by the Kofila, with his servants, and followed it slowly to Azoad, from which his two letters are dated.

Here he found Marabout Mooktar, who treated him kindly, and promised him every assistance in prosecuting his journey; but, unluckily, a dangerous epidemic fever raged in the place, which carried off half the population, including Baboni and the friendly Mooktar. It proved fatal to all Laing's servants, except Hamet, and he himself suffered from it severely. The death of Baboni delayed the Kofila for a considerable time at Azoad.

On February 20 1827, letters were brought by courier from Ghadamis to Tripoli, stating on the authority of oral report, that Major Laing was in Timbuctoo in good health and spirits; but the bashaw, at the request of the British consul, having directed special inquiries to be made, further accounts were received on March 31. According to these, the appearance of the Christian in Timbuctoo had excited the prejudices of the powerful tribe of the Fellata, who had threatened to plunder the town if he was not sent away. The people of the town then gave him a guide, with whom he set out for Bambarra, but the fellata overtook him on the road, and murdered him.

one brief generation, under the Abbasid Khadifs, it eclipsed Baghdad and was one of the brilliant capitals of the world. These results alone would have given distinction to a remarkable journey and importance to an admirable book.

Miss Bell describes her aim in the prefatory letter to Lord Cromer. Along the eastern edge of the Syrian desert, where many more massive skeletons of forgotten cities may yet be found amid unexplored regions of the sand, Miss Bell had determined to follow the footsteps of Chesney and Layard and the rest:

'Not only would I set myself to trace the story that was scored upon the face of the earth by mouldering wall or half-choked dyke, by the thousand vestiges of former culture, scattered about my path, but I would attempt to record the daily life and speech of those who had inherited this empty ground whereon Empires had risen and expired'.

That is the contrast which makes the double interest of *Amurath to Amurath.* It is the most solid of Miss Gertrude Bell's books. It is legitimately ambitious, for it makes a notable contribution to archaeology. This weights some parts of it a good deal, and the general reader will wish now and then that there were less evidence of eastern learning and of architectural knowledge. Arabic accents and Squinch arches are a little of a weariness to the flesh.

But then there is also the human side. Miss Bell travelled through the remoter provinces of the Ottoman Empire in 1909, the year completing the glorious revolution. She came to appreciate the extraordinary difference in the point of view that separates the populations in the Asiatic vilayets from the Young Turks on the Bosphorus. These pages have a high political value as a life-like picture of an unparalleled phase of experience in the East. In Muslim cities, Arab tents and Christian monasteries she discoursed upon the idea and prospects of 'liberty.' The verdicts were curious, disquieting, and of profound interest. Miss Bell records these talks in colloquial form as they took place, and with all her vivacious skill she has never been more entertaining than in the social and picturesque chapters of this narrative. Even those who may find the archaeological sections too solid and technical will be enchanted with rest. As a record of dead cities and living conversations – of the ruins of old despotisms that were long before the Turk and of the wild pulsings of wonder and fanaticism after the fall of Abdul Hamid – the book is lit and shadowed by a fascinating interplay of scenes and emotions.

The tale begins in the bazaar of Aleppo with brisk chaffering for a hank of string. Presently a party of dyers gave their opinion on the political situation:

'"Christian and Muslim," said one, "see how we labour! If the constitution were worth anything, the poor would not work for such small rewards."

"At any rate," said I, "you get your namualyeh (whatever that is) cheaper this year."

"Eh, true," he replied, "but who can tell how long that will last?"

"Please God it will endure," said I.

"Please God," he answered, "but we should have been better satisfied to see the soldiers govern. A strong hand we need here in Aleppo, that the poor may enjoy the fruits of their toil.'

"Eh, wah!" said another, "and a Government that we know!" '

That note was echoed to the end. The Asiatic vilayets wanted not liberty in the Western sense, but government. They would have applauded Seeley and taken him literally had he said to them as to us that liberty means the right man in the right place. But, again:

' "How can there be liberty under Islam?" said a white-bearded sheikh of the tents. "Shall I take a wife contrary to the laws of Islam and call it liberty? God forbid." '

More illuminating still was the talk with a Muslim gentleman in the town of Deir. He refused to join any Committee of Progress. 'I am lord over much business,' said he, 'but they are the fathers of idle talk.' There was a general agreement that the Turks understood government – while as yet the Arabs, intelligent and restive as they are, only understand anarchy – and things which humanitarians and others in the west might be tempted to call atrocities were quoted on the Euphrates as proofs of the ruling capacity of the dominant race. Miss Bell sums up with a mind-clearing thing:-

'Thus it is through all the Asiatic provinces, and the further I went the more convinced did I become that the European Turkey is the head and brain of the empire, and that if the difficult task of reform is to be carried out in Asia it can only come from western Turkey. I believe that this had been recognised in Constantinople, for the provincial governors appointed under the new regime have been almost invariably well chose.'

Yet from Aleppo, down the Euphrates, to Baghdad, and up the Tigris again to the Armenian mountains, how thin are the partitions that divide all daily life from tyranny, extortion, and massacre. But let us turn to the more entertaining and perhaps not less instructive topics. Miss Bell is a happy reporter of travel talk, and among the political colloquies there are social conversations on wives and motor cars and the evil eye:

'The smell of the waste seized us as we passed beyond the sulphur marshes. Hussein Onbashi held his head higher, and we gave each other the salaam anew.

"At Hit," said he, and his words went far to explain the lightness of his heart, "I have left three wives in the house."

"Mashallah," said Fattah, "you must be deaf with the gir-gir-gir of them."

"Eh, billah," assented Hussein, "I shut my ears. Twenty children have I had and seven wives; three of these died and one left me and returned to her own people. But I shall take another bride this year, please God."

"We Christians," said Fattah, "find one enough."

"You may be right," answered Hussein politely, "yet I would take a new wife every year, if I had the means."'

Nor can we ignore the story of the evil eye if we want to understand how much in the immemorial psychology of the East is as yet left unchanged by political revolutions:

' "And if Your Excellency doubts," said Fattah, "I can tell you that there is a man we'd known in Aleppo, who has one good eye and one evil. And this he keeps bound under a kerchief. And, one day when he was sitting in the house of friends they said to him, 'Why do you bind up the left eye?' He said, 'It is an evil eye.' Then they said, 'If you were to take off the kerchief and look at the lamp hanging from the roof, would it fall?' 'Without doubt,' said he, and with that he unbound the kerchief and looked, and the lamp fell to the ground." "Allah," said Fawwaz. "There is a man at who has never dared to look at his own son."'

We have been tempted to let extracts run beyond measure, but there are heaps of wise and vivid things that we would like to quote were space unlimited. There is the admirable passage reminding us that 'Islam is like a great sounding board stretched across Asia: every voice goes up to it and reverberates back; every judgment pronounced in anger, every misrepresentation, comes down from it magnified a thousand-fold.' Nothing in connection with our imperial politics is more necessary to remember. And still we have said nothing about the talks with these bright and respectable folk the devil-worshippers, or with monks of ancient Christian sects still clinging centuries after the fall of Julian and the apparition of Islam to their mountain eyries. What a wonderful region of the world it is this cradle of all the greater faiths; and Miss Bell is by long odds the ablest and bravest Englishwoman who has invaded the Arab desert since the more eccentric and dilettante days of Lady Hester Stanhope.

JL Garvin

Across the Sahara by caterpillar

Observer, January 14 1923

The feat of the French Expedition which has just crossed the middle of the Sahara in cars is one of the most remarkable in the records of African discovery. To have cut down the time taken over the journey from Algeria to Timbuctoo from an average of six or seven months to 20 days is a very fine achievement, and the two Frenchmen who led the expedition deserve the congratulations of the whole world.

Of these two one is an expert motor engineer and a keen explorer of the desert. Monsieur G. M. Haardt is the manager of the Citroen car works; and Lieutenant Louis Audouin-Dubreuil, who, during the war was an officer in the French Flying Corps, has a great love of the vast horizons of the Sahara, on the seaward margin of which he has built himself a house. Two other members of the party were M. Paul Castelnan, a geographer of some distinction, and Lieutenant Estienne, whose father (General Estienne) was responsible for the French tanks during the war.

But, allowing for the suitability and efficiency of these four chief members of the eight who formed the expedition, their combined skill and knowledge could not have availed against the conditions of Saharan travel without something superior to any ordinary car or caterpillar. The factor which enabled the four cars to maintain an average speed of over 112 miles a day was the amazingly clever invention known as the Kegresse-Hinstin caterpillar. This consists of an endless band of heavy rubber held in place by a broad articulated flange running on two pulley wheels which are not rigidly attached to the chassis of the car. The front pair only rest on the ground by their own weight, and rise and fall as they encounter any object, and the space between the front and back pulleys (the latter drive the endless bands) is filled with four small roller wheels. These are arranged in pairs, each working on very supple springs attached to the main axle.

Thus not only does the whole plane of each caterpillar alter according to the surface presented, but it presents a great length of yielding surface which undulates over rocks, stones, ledges, and other irregularities without any real interference with the propulsive power of the drive. Instead, therefore, of crawling along at three or four miles an hour, the car fitted with this most clever invention moves with a rapidity which has now been tested for three weeks in the severest conditions.

If the experience of this first journey by the new means of propulsion implies that roads are not an essential feature of travel in the Sahara, we are seeing the first streak of a new dawn which will dissipate the gloom of ignorance hitherto obscuring this great zone of Africa. In the first place adequate surveys for the best routes for road engineering can be made with speed and safety. Following this will come the work of sinking wells in likely places – generally in the old river beds – and at each the establishment of a small military post with its own caterpillar cars which will enable small flying columns to move rapidly against any 'rezzou,' or nomadic marauding parties mounted on camels. By this means the days of the desert robber bands will be numbered. Unable to reach the very few wells, their movements will be more and more restricted and the desert will offer less and less in the way of plunder.

Major Gordon Home

British women's adventures in Gobi and Turkestan

Guardian, May 5 1927

A remarkable story of a journey made from the north-west province of China (Kansu) across the desert of Gobi (Chinese Turkestan) to Omsk, in Siberia, is told by three British women who have recently come back to England. They are Miss Mildred Cable and the Misses Eva and Francesca French, whose services to the China Inland mission, to which they belong, vary from 19 to 34 years. They have been spending some time in Switzerland before engaging on a speaking tour of this country.

'Suchow, where we have been living for some time, is 450 miles beyond the last mission station in China, at Lanchow,' Miss Cable told me. 'It lies just at the end of the Great Wall, and is on the direct caravan route into China from central Asia. This is the route followed by Marco Polo, whose name is still remembered in the area. We decided to come home via Russia, and our journey to Omsk took us four months, travelling about 30 miles a day by mule cart with two Chinese servants. We were the first British women ever to traverse this route, but we had a splendid reception everywhere.'

'We had a narrow escape from brigands and also had to exist for many days on brackish water,' said Miss Francesca French. 'One of the most pitiful sights we saw were the White Russian emigrés who have had to join the ranks of Chinese beggars. Some of the women have become subsidiary wives to Chinese, and the tragedies we met with were appalling. Not a little of the lowering of western prestige in the eyes of the Chinese is due to the condition of these emigrés.'

As the party crossed into Siberia it had to leave all printed matter behind. The three ladies were held up for some time in the city of Semipalatinsk by the authorities. Finally, however, they were given the fullest help by a Jewish gentleman who spoke perfect English. He admitted he had been put to watch them to discover the purpose of their visit, especially because of their arrival from such an unexpected quarter.

Secrets of the Arabian desert
(edited from a sequence of five articles)

Guardian, February 1931

My camel journey of 900 miles across the Rub' al Khali took 58 days, 13 halted, 45 marching, averaging eight hours a day in the saddle. I travelled in Arab kit, but otherwise as an undisguised Christian. In my baggage were a prismatic compass, sextant, and navigational instruments for mapping purposes. The starting point was Dhufar, a central point on the South Arabian coast, and I set out with an escort of 30 Arabs and 40 camels. When I arrived at Doha in the Persian Gulf, the escort numbered 13 Arabs and 18 camels, having been progressively reduced as the early menace of Hadramaut raiders was left behind. The route lay north over the Qara mountains, 3,000 feet in altitude, through the frankincense country of the Bible, across the steppe I explored last winter to Shisur, and thence westwards into the unknown. For 100 waterless miles I skirted the southern edge of the sands, mighty bulwarks of red, fringed with dunes, the habitat of ostrich and antelope, the former now almost extinct, the latter plentiful – I am bringing a young calf to England.

In latitude 19 deg longitude 52 deg, we came upon numerous deep-cut caravan tracks in patches of steppe running across our path, evidence of centuries of usage in bygone times. The bedouin call it the road to Ubar; their legendary city of prehistoric days. The sands have in the course of the ages encroached southwards, and hereabouts lies Ubar, according to local tribesmen, buried beneath them, the Atlantis of the Rub' al Khali. These borderlands, 100 miles from the sea and 1,000 feet in altitude, are strewn with seashell fossils.

Proceeding north-west, we encountered the phenomenon of singing sands; a deep, sustained booming caused by the wind action among the sand cliffs, and resembling the note of a ship's siren. In latitude 19 longitude 50deg 45min I turned northwards, and so continued through the midmost heart of the sands, where we encountered sandstorms, which my small cine camera and one aneroid did not survive. I carried no tent from considerations of weight. The night temperatures averaged 50 degrees, falling to below 40 on occasion.

North of the 23rd parallel the altitude falls to the sea level, and actually below it, where I discovered a lake of salt water seven miles long. West of my line of march the sands were reported to me to be rising in altitude and waterless. East of it the sands fall and water is extremely plentiful – a veritable sub-surface lake, so brackish in parts, however, as to be undrinkable by man and sometimes even by camel. The whole region appears to have been beneath the sea in late geological times.

The inhabitants of the sands are scant nomad sections of the Al-Kathi and Al-Murra tribes, subsisting exclusively on camels' milk. Of wild animal life, the raven is the most persistent bird, the bustard is widespread, and I collected eagle's eggs. Fox, hare, and lizards are common, wolves, wild cat, and all mammals are of the light-sand colour of their environment, in contrast to the herds of black Murra camels. The expedition made possible the mapping of names and the location of sands and wells, and the collection of geological and other natural history specimens and of meteorological data.

On Christmas Eve we turned more northwards, and stuck into the body of the sands, leaving their southern edge stretching away in a west-south-westerly direction. Gone were the fair and gentle corridors. Before us rose red mountains of sand. The scene was almost Alpine in character, and glorious vistas rewarded us from the high places, vistas of immense peaks to which small isolated camel thorn and their own pure colour lent an air of exaggerated size. Below them often appeared lake-like expanses of white, which on closer inspection proved to be but more examples of the gypsum patches met with in the past few days.

Christmas Eve was to be a night of excitement. We had arrived late in camp, camels had been hobbled as usual and shooed off to the scant bushes from behind some of which came the brisk noises of merry camp fire parties. A sudden scream. To me it was like the hooting of an owl or whining of some beast. There was an immediate 'hurroosli.'

'Gom! Gom!' 'Raiders, raiders,' shouted excitable Badus, leaping to their feet, their rifles at the ready, and my servant came running across to me with my Winchester and bandolier. Our rabias, of the Awamir and Karab tribes, rushed out in their several directions and began shouting: 'We are alert! We are alert! I am Abu Fulan (So-and-So), of such and such a tribe. These are my party and are under my protection.'

The object of this was to save us from raiders of his own faction, if these they were. I gathered that the cry is never abused. I was thoroughly tired and hence well disposed to believe that the alarm had been raised by a wild beast and not an enemy, so that my vigil fell short of that of my companions. My assumption was correct. Next morning the tracks of a wolf were traced near by; its whoop had, it seemed, been suspiciously like the Awan, the war-cry of raiders in the final act.

Bertram Thomas

A golden journey: In Arabia Felix.

Observer, May 31 1936

The Southern Gates of Arabia, by Freya Stark (John Murray, 18s)

The right, the only way, to begin a review of this book that might do justice to it would be by a quotation. That much I realised before I had finished the introduction, the pedestrian name given to one of the most moving beginnings to a book I have had the good luck to read. And then, as I read on, in every page more captured by a story and a manner of telling it such as you come across once is a lifetime, I saw that I could not choose that quotation. A score of paper slips mark the pages where I read, and read again, passages that stand out like the crimson roses in the pattern of a Bokhara tapestry, but I cannot find one that is lovelier than another, fitter to give you a notion of the distinction of this simple record.

That is only a half-truth. I cannot find a single passage that will do, but I have lost count of how many would be needed to show you what a tale is here, what humour, wit, kindliness, what unstudied restraint in the telling. The author uses words in a way that falls on your mind like music, in sequences that bury themselves in your memory like staves; yet you will not find one that is not part of our common speech, to be read every day in book and newspaper. You read her book very jealously, sentence by sentence, phrase by phrase, going back again and again to them lest you miss some indefinable essential of the grace of her writing.

It is a simple record, simply told, and in that lies its compelling strength. You read of people and things and places that must be new to you and to all but a handful of explorers who went a little of the way Miss Stark rode, and in the reading you look with new eyes upon a world you remember only in dreams. As you slowly turn and turn back the pages, lingering over every episode, every sharp-cut sketch, you realise that here at last you are reading the story on which the dreams of every traveller in the East are built, no cloudy foundations of fancy, but the solid rock of truth.

Miss Stark went to the Hadhramaut, at the southern end of Arabia, with the hope of reaching the city of Shabwa, until now unvisited. In that matchless introduction she explains, without a word of explanation, why she yielded to a passion for roads and rivers, and went alone into a country whose record in the history of the nations and their commerce in the eternal luxuries goes back to the beginning of time, a country lying close upon the course of all the ships that have ever sailed to the East, that has been passed by on the other side by nearly all the travellers of the world.

Hear her in that first part which, if you please, is called 'The Incense Road':

'Here [the frankincense country] Arab camelmen waited under the dust of their camps as they do now, and in their bales, together with the incense of Arabia and Africa, tied pearls and muslins from Ceylon and silks from China, Malacca tortoise-shell and spikenard from the Ganges. Himalayan cinnamon leaves, called Malabathrum.

'coronates nitentes

'malobathro syrio capillos.

'And from India, diamonds and sapphires, ivory and cotton, lapis lazuli, and cinnamon and pepper above all. And dates and wine, gold and slaves from the Persian Gulf; and from the eastern coast of Africa, long subject to Arabian traders, frankincense, gold and myrrh, ivory and ostrich feathers and oil.'

Gold and slaves and wine … peals and spikenard … ivory, dates and oil. Words we know, but not with all that treasure of suggestion.

'This was the great frankincense road whose faint remembrance still gives to South Arabia the name of Happy; whose existence prepared and made possible the later exploits of Islam. On its stream of padding feet the riches of Asia travelled; along its slow continuous thread the Arabian empires rose and fell ...'

The RAF has landing places in that lonely country, but its machines are the only and rare visitors. You might think that some account of the difficulties might not only be excusable but expected. Travellers tell tales by right. Not Miss Stark, for whom difficulties are another side of her happiness. She just tells you that she took passage in a little steamer from Aden to Makalla, and in a casual sentence lights up a background of piracy and wrecking, of oriental bargaining at its most purple. And the ambassador charged with the highly delicate negotiations between the putative owner of a wrecked cargo and its actual possessor was travelling in the same little steamer, with his aunt – 'singularly beautiful for an aunt,' says Miss Stark – who relied upon buttery pastry as a cure for seasickness and, when the ship rode at anchor in blessed immobility, still banged upon the intervening bulkhead at frequent intervals to demand the solace of company.

To the ship came at last the police, in a boat 'swishing like a black shark in the path of the moonlight' and in leisurely course of time Miss Stark was landed for her adventures. She does not think of them as adventures, the first Christian woman to make that strange journey, but, so it seems to me as I read her, as agreeable decorations on the smooth pattern of life. Everything fills her with a deep pleasure, from the primitive beauty of the people to the harsh magnificence of the scenery. Wherever she goes she makes friends who take her into their intimate confidence with a generosity that is seldom met with in the more accessible parts of the East.

In the cities, some a huddle of houses in the sand, some white ancient towns, 'leaning against the cliff face' with all the dignity and splendour of empire, Miss Stark stayed as the honoured guest of high officialdom of every rank and order, and her accounts of life in the harem are delightful. She fell gravely ill of measles, which seems to be a pestilince of Arabia, but you would think she regarded the whole grim business as an interesting interlude, an opportunity for studying Eastern customs in the sick room, rather than as a disaster – except in so far as the consequences of her illness prevented her reaching her goal.

Scented soap is considered a contributory cause of measles in the Hadhramaut, but Miss Stark's hosts were anxious to cure her by means of a hot iron applied to the neck. She dodged this, but not the sorceress who came and, after invocations and the untying of countless knots in her shawl (strictly forbidden in the Koran), spat on her. It was kindly meant, says the patient.

She lay in that upper chamber incapable of movement, aching in every bone and in a high fever, watching from her window 'the motionless cliffs, their pure and sharp outline and the shadow that falls and rises on their sides with the steps of the sun, like a bucket in a well, measuring out the days.'

The entrancing tale moves unhurriedly forward, step by step, and as you read you find yourself at peace with all the world.

John Priolea

Desert Elegy

Observer, October 25 1959

Arabian Sands, by Wilfred Thesiger (Longmans, 35s)

Mr Wilfred Thesiger is the last of a distinguished line of travellers to whom we owe the exploration of Arabia. Since the middle of the last century the exploration has been mainly an English affair. With the exception of Musil, the foremost names are English: Burton, Palgrave, Doughty, Thomas and Philby. Now there is Mr Thesiger. Many believe, Mr St John Philby with characteristic generosity is among them, that he is the greatest of the explorers.

While still an undergraduate Mr Thesiger ventured alone into the heart of the Danakil country and was one of the first white men to do so and emerge alive. Later, when a political officer in the Sudan, where for a time he served in unconventional fashion, he travelled among the Dinkas, and in the course of another solitary expedition, this time to Tibesti in the central Sahara, covered over 2,000 miles by camel. These and other journeys, considerable achievements in themselves, proved a preparation for the southern deserts of Arabia, the desolate Empty Quarter of which Doughty wrote, 'I never found an Arabian who had aught to tell, even by hearsay, of that dreadful country.' In the 30s two Englishmen, Bertram Thomas and Mr St John Philby, succeeded in crossing it, but it still remained, when Mr Thesiger set out on the first of his epic journeys in 1946, perhaps the last considerable area in the world of which the world knew almost nothing.

Many who have celebrated the Arabian deserts have written with distinction. Even if Doughty had not elaborated his masterpiece, the region would have been ill served by the books of travellers. Mr Thesiger's *Arabian Sands* can take its place in an impressive tradition. The style is stripped, bare almost to a fault, yet rightly so for it well conveys the discipline of the environment, the taxing camel stages, the movement across the empty map. It has the dignity of scrupulous writing. The appalling hardships, the strange exhilaration, of these journeys, undertaken barefoot, on camel back, with two or three devoted Bedu companions, are recorded with a truth that will make them read as well in 50 years as they do today.

Of its nature a good travel book is the account both of a journey and a person. There is no doubt of the author's stature as it is revealed, all unconsciously, in *Arabian Sands*. He looms large even in the expanses of the Empty Quarter and seems impressive in ways that are not contemporary. For all the differences, not least in style, Doughty cannot but come to mind as one reads. The interest of the book is thus, apart from the achievements recorded, the interest of the man. Whether he is describing the monstrous sand dunes of the Uruq al Shaiba, or the 16 days' waterless transit to the well at Hassi, or speaking of the Bedu civilisation which he so loves and understands, one is aware of convictions that are unrepresentative of our time and a viewpoint that dispenses with our values.

The author's character and attitude give *Arabian Sands* a significance that has nothing to do with exploration. The perceptive reader will discover that the book is an indictment, all the more telling because rarely explicit, of Western civilisation. Mr Thesiger's desert was 'very still with the silence which we have driven from our world,' and after five years journeying as Bedu, and with Bedu, he recalled on leaving their sere peninsula, perhaps above all else, how often he had been humbled by the illiterate herdsmen who possessed, he felt, in so much greater measure than himself generosity and courage, endurance and patience. It would be reasonable to regard Mr Thesiger as a man notably endowed by the standards of the west with most of these virtues. *Arabian Sands* is a disturbing book.

In a sense it is also a sad book, for it inevitably strikes an elegiac note, if elegy can be expressed in such terse prose. Mr Thesiger saw the arrival of the first oil technicians and he knows that Bedu life is doomed. The men who for centuries have preferred spare existence on the fringes of the Empty Quarter to ease in the richer settled lands (that they could so easily have occupied) are now to have comfort thrust upon them. The travelling salesman will replace the traveller, the aeroplane will supersede the camel. There will be many more books about Arabia, but they will not be able to speak of an Empty Quarter or tell of men such as those with whom Mr Thesiger journeyed.

Robin Fedden

Going to extremes

Guardian, March 28 1974

The Fearful Void, by Geoffrey Moorhouse (Hodder & Stoughton, £3.50)

The great Victorian explorers would have thought Geoffrey Moorhouse mad. He submitted himself to dangers, hardships and discomforts as horrible as theirs but for no apparent reason. No lakes, mountains and rivers awaited discovery, no geographical riddles invited solution, no fame was to be won. Why, then, with blistered feet, louse-infested garments and rebellious bowels, trudge across 2,000 miles of dreadful desert, only now and then mounting a despondent camel?

If cross the Sahara you must, there are several age-old, well-worn routes from north to south with water, filling stations, trucks and buses, and overhead planes taking politicians to conferences and pilgrims to Mecca. There is no point in going from west to east and no established trade routes, just sand and rocks and wells and nomads, the Empty Quarter of Africa.

'It was because I was afraid that I had decided to attempt a crossing of the great Sahara desert, from west to east, by myself and by camel.' Mr Moorhouse believes that all of us live in a permanent state of fear of one kind or another: of pain and death only rarely, of making a fool of oneself, of being rebuffed, of ridicule, of failure, almost all of the time. This fear he set out to exorcise by provoking it, as one might summon a dragon from its lair in order to slay it. A strange thing for a middle-aged journalist with a wife and children – he spent his 41st birthday in the desert – to do, but in the grain of his nature. In *Calcutta* he investigated extremes of urban pressures, in this venture he investigates what extremes of solitude and hardship can do to a man, starting with himself. A masochistic exercise, very much of our time. It is not the desert Mr Moorhouse sets out to explore but the effect of the desert on his own personality.

His intention to travel quite alone was a dead duck from the start but he took only one companion at a time, with several changes. These were nomads and Muslims, all Arab-speaking except the last, and nicest, who was a Tuareg. He found the others mostly mean, grasping, arrogant, dirty and incompetent, carelessly capsizing water bags when death from thirst stared them in the face. Also they were tough, devout, generally uncomplaining and, while they swindled their employer whenever they could, they did not abandon him, or slit his throat for his wealth.

His journey ended in failure. His aim was to plod from Nouakchott on the Atlantic across Mauretania, Mali, southern Algeria and Egypt to the Nile, a distance of 3,500 miles, but he was forced to give up at Tamanrasset in Algeria with another 1,500 miles to go. Only a doggedness and guts extraordinary in a middle-aged civilised modern man kept him going across 2,000 miles of rock and sand and burning heat guided by compass and the stars – his sextant suffered damage near the start. The food, when there was any, was revolting, suppurating sores and lice tormented him, chronic dysentery set in and when, near Tomboukto, his will power cracked, only his companion's bullying forced him on.

I once knew of a young man who went down a ladder in a disused mineshaft, padlocked himself to the rungs and threw away the key. His skeleton was found years later. Mr Moorhouse went down the ladder as far as he could but fortunately without the padlock and he climbed back, thinking of the two women in his life, of his children and of Christmas shopping in Oxford street. He has brought back his discoveries; how much his body can stand and how far his will power can control it, how people behave under extreme hardship, how trivial are the voices of our own gods and how silent those of sand and stars where men are nothing.

His book ends with a visit to the mountain retreat where Charles de Foucard, ex-soldier, roué explorer and finally Christian mystic, had his hermitage and simple chapel. Here Mr Moorhouse offered his equally simple thanks for survival. As, on another plane, we may do for a very honest book, simply told, explicit, every word of it lived through with nothing that is secondhand. It rings true. In a world that is shrinking to a chain of Hiltons linked by fleets of coaches, travel books seem doomed unless related to a specialist topic. Geoffrey Moorhouse's topic is the nature of man.

Elspeth Huxley

Sands of time

Guardian, February 8 1975

The journey was heroic, and so was the style of the invective. Meet the schoolmaster, 'a depraved, fanatical young man … sordid was his voice, and the baseness of his snake-looking eyes a moral pestilence.' The schoolmaster remains forever memorable because he ran foul of one of the great Victorian travellers, the first to systematically explore the central Arabian deserts, virtually unarmed and penniless, living hand-to-mouth with the bedouin nomads.

It is now a century since Charles Montagu Doughty, then a 32-year-old geologist with aspirations to poetry began his journeys in the desert with a camel ride alone through Sinai to investigate monuments at Maan and Petra. It was there that he heard of ancient, pre-Islamic inscriptions in the southern deserts: to visit them would be impossible for a penniless

Christian, but he decided to go anyway. Without help from any learned society or official body he set out again in 1876 with the Haj camel train on the Mecca pilgrimage. Medain Salih was as near to the sacred city as he could do, and at that point he turned left, relying for his survival on exploiting the rigid bedouin codes governing the treatment of hearth guests and road companions.

He came back two years later with some of the first detailed maps of north-west Arabia (in 1921 the War Office wanted his notes for their five miles to the inch maps of the Hejaz and Jebel Shammar), the first records of ancient Arabic inscriptions in the peninsular (edited by Renan and published in 1884), and a monumental 500,000-word traveller's tale which TE Lawrence was later to compare with Marco Polo.

Four publishers rejected the manuscript of *Travels in Arabia Deserta* before it was published by Cambridge University Press in 1888. One of them felt that it ought to be 'practically rewritten by a practised literary man', which was insensitive but forgivable, because Doughty certainly did not write short clipped sentences in the manner later adopted by Lord Beaverbrook. (He would have been at one with the Beaver in his championing of the English word against the foreign one: Doughty disliked words like 'photograph' and coined instead 'lightprint' or 'flameprint').

The son of a Suffolk parson, he had graduated from Cambridge in geology but later immersed himself in 16th century literature and Teutonic languages because he wanted to 'recall the legendary beginnings of the British race in verse which should revive the dictions of Chaucer and Spenser.' Thus the *Dictionary of National Biography*, but another critic remarked that he used the English language as if it was

Wilfrid Thesiger

just something he had found lying around, with no knowledge of its tradition or antecedents.

But he had what travel writers need most, which is a feeling for place. When you ride with Doughty you can see the basins, crests, cones and ridges ahead and feel the baked sandstone, flint, pumice, granite, limestone and basalt underfoot. No bald catalogues either: '...an iron desolation; what uncouth blackness and cumber of volcanic matter! an hard-set face of nature without a smile forever, a wilderness of burning and rusty horror of unformed matter.' You know the people he rides with, his rafiks or road companions, bound to him by the code of mutual protection: their ignorance, their kindliness, their savagery, their distress at being trapped into sharing the road with a Christian, a Nazarene, a Nasrany.

Most of Doughty's troubles sprang from Islam, 'that dreadful-faced harpy of their religion.' He rode through Arabia wearing his Christianity like Bunyan's Mr Standfast. He was exhorted time and again by new-won bedouin friends to style himself a Muslim 'and in my heart be still of what opinion I would ... but I could not find it in my life to confess the barbaric prophet of Mecca and enter, under the yoke, into their solemn fools' paradise.'

He grubbed what income he could, practising as a doctor, but found that being an honest physician paid few dividends: 'He who would thrive must resemble them, some glozing Asiatic that can file his tongue to the baseness of those Semitic minds.' But his plain speaking made him friends, too, often among desert dwellers who were themselves far from home – discharged soldiers of the Ottoman empire who had been recruited in Morocco, Albania, Kurdistan in southern Russia; a free Galla negro captured as a child in Abyssinia.

If the invective is superb, the merriment in *Arabia Deserta* is sparse. He was living like the desert peoples, a chronicle of blood-feud and brigandage. He warns: 'I pray nothing be looked for in this book but the seeing of a hungry man and the telling of a most weary man.' Almost the only fun (and dry fun at that) comes from his attempts to explain England to his new found friends. He told one how 'for a fox brush, sheyks in my beled used to ride furiously in red mantles upon horses... and the good-Medina Moslem seemed to muse in spirit 'Wherefore had the Lord endowed the Nasara with a superfluity of riches to make so idles uses."

He made his way to the court of Ibn Rashid at Hayil in the Jebel Shammar (where, marvellously, he met an Italian planning to bluff his way into Mecca and then write a book about it), and doggedly faced the suspicion, distrust, ambition, ignorance and curiosity of the desert princes. 'In our talk he inquired of those marvellous things of the Narara, the telegraph, and glass... and Baris (Paris), a city builded [sic] all of crystal, also what thing was rock oil?'

He sensed Hamlet-like tragedies to be written in the bloody rise of Ibn Rashid, horrible confusion of wedlock and parricide and pre-emptive butchery and of the seed of murder planted in the young; of a child of sad orphan looks whom Doughty heard say to himself: ' 'Ha – it was he who killed such an one or other' – and the horrible word seemed to be of presage, it was so light on the child's lips – O God! Who can forecast their tragedies to come! What shall be the next vengeance and succession and forestalling of deaths between them?'

His health shattered by his privations, Doughty went home, married, wrote *Arabia Deserta* and then six volumes of blank verse at Tunbridge Wells and Eastbourne and then died at Sissinghurst in 1926. CUP printed only 240 copies of *Arabia Deserta* and by 1920 it fetched a secondhand value of £30. TE Lawrence thought it the best travel book in the world 'not dull at all, but in a queer style that demands care at first,' and persuaded Jonathan Cape to republish. Cape reprinted the work several times between 1921 and the war, and Penguin brought out an abridgement by Edward Garnett. For all that, the work remains only slightly better know than Doughty's poems, the preserve of the Arabist and the old-fashioned bookworm. Cape say they have no plans to republish.

Tim Radford

Hunt-the-robyn, a desert game

Guardian, August 27 1977

The Lady of the Camels (*Guardian*), the Young Woman Desert Walker (*Daily Telegraph*), or the Camel Lady of the Gibson Desert (*Daily Mail*) is obviously a brave woman. Not so much by virtue of her feat in crossing the 2,000 miles of the Gibson Desert in Australia by camel, but more by her courage in coping with the ballyhoo (*Concise Oxford Dictionary*: 'trumped-up publicity of a vulgar or misleading kind') that has already greeted her exploits. Perhaps courage is not the right word: cunning, or ingenuity rather, for having already been the victim of the outriders of the civilised world as she reached journey's end Miss Robyn Davidson is now thought to be heading away from the small town of Wiluna where the rest of the media men await her. Indeed, she had already sought to sweep away her tracks so that she could hide from the first white hunters in search of her but alas her camels' tracks were found by an alert Aboriginal tracker named Johnny Long. And so, we gather, she was at last flushed out of the porcupine grass in which she was hiding. A man from the *Daily Mail* was in the flushing-out party. 'Johnny ... led me through heavy desert scrub to the small blonde figure huddled over a fire to keep out the cold of the breaking dawn.' Mercifully the *Mail* reporter refrained from saying, 'Miss Davidson, I presume.' Otherwise he laid it on pretty thick. Miss Davidson has not worn make-up for months, makes her tea in a billy, chews nuts and berries, had to kill six attacking bull camels, and told the *Mail* man: 'It's not a personal endurance test. It is simply me getting away from all that junk out there, the TV sets, the cars, the lanes, and getting right back to nature.'

Alas civilisation has already caught up with the Camel Lady. There will be plenty of people who might share Miss Davidson's philosophy, but lack the time, the desert, the camels or the courage to emulate her. They might even cheer her on if, having sampled civilisation again, she headed straight back into the desert with her camels the way she came. Then at least she could enjoy another three months away from 'all that junk out there' and – yes, we might as well say it – from latter-day HM Stanleys too.

Leader

Going for a Burton

Guardian, September 19 1998

A Rage to Live: A Biography of Richard and Isabel Burton by Mary S Lovell (Little, Brown, £25)

If a book were written with the title 'Disreputable Victorians', the chief of them would be this fabulous beast of a man – Dirty Dick, Ruffian Dick, Sir Richard Burton: explorer, linguist, diplomat, pornographer. He was the bad boy's bad boy, a hard drinking, hard fighting fornicator who was also one of the most remarkable scholars of the 19th century.

'Pious mothers loathed Burton's name, and even men of the world mentioned it apologetically,' according to a fellow member of the Royal Geographical Society, so a book which offers the story not just of adventurous Richard, but of his wife Isabel is a treat indeed. Burton started to attract his formidable reputation when he was an officer in the Indian army where his Indian friends and mistresses earned him the sobriquet 'white nigger' among brother officers and a reputation for immorality such that when he buried his beloved gamecock in his garden, word went round it was a baby's grave.

Already a considerable linguist, in the Bombay Infantry he added Hindustani, Gujerati, Maratha, Persian, Sindi and Punjabi to the tongues he had already mastered – he was eventually fluent in 29 languages. He even installed forty monkeys in his house and attempted to compile a vocabulary of 'monkey language'. His spying missions where he went disguised as a native developed into personal explorations, including his famous trip to Mecca as a bogus pilgrim for which, in an extreme act of subterfuge, he had himself circumcised.

Yet Burton's daring and scholarship did not make him popular. As a contemporary wrote, he was not feared for what he did, 'but for what he was believed capable of doing, and also for the reserve of power and that unspoken sense of superiority which the dullest and vainest could scarcely fail to feel in his presence'.

One of the many conundrums of his life is how this buccaneering, wild man could end up with the simperingly religious Isabel Burton. Mary Lovell's position is that there is no conundrum: Isabel Burton has been traduced by earlier biographers and in fact was a buccaneering, adventuring spirit herself. She was a passionate woman who declared on first seeing Burton, 'That man will marry me', and who learned fencing in order to be better able to protect him when danger struck. She too yearned to be released from 'respectability – the harness of European society'. When she joined him in taking up a consular position in Damascus she enthused, 'I shall have tents, horses, weapons, and be free …'

It was love at first sight, or it was for her, anyway. When Burton eventually proposed, and asked if she wanted some time to think it over, she replied, 'I do not want to think it over. I have been thinking it over for six years, ever since I first saw you at Boulogne. I have prayed for you every morning and night, I have followed your career minutely, I have read every word you ever wrote, and I would rather have a crust and a tent with you than be queen of all the world.' So he took that as a 'yes'. Her mother was less easy to please, and told Isabel she would give consent for her to marry any man on earth rather than Richard Burton.

The long wait for this love to be consummated provides half the narrative interest of the book. The other is the way in which Burton was cheated out of full recognition for his part in the discovery of the source of the Nile. Burton was stimulated to seek the source by a line from Ptolemy's *Geographica* – 'the lakes whence the Nile flows'.

To find those lakes struck him as a way of making his name forever. He took John Hanning Speke along with him, a poor choice of companion as Speke had few appropriate abilities, his main interest in Africa being to see how many exotic animals he could shoot. Unbeknown to his companion in the extreme hardships of the journey, this big-game hunter had also got Richard Burton in his sights. Speke left Burton, who was too sick to travel, at a base camp in the lake region to lead a party north to investigate the lakes, returning to declare (with utterly insufficient evidence) that he had found the source of the Nile. When they were both back at the East African coast, Speke took off to Britain, promising he would not go to the Royal Geographical Society until Burton had joined him. Of course, that is exactly what he did, using his head start to garner the laurels for the discovery to himself alone.

Speke was one of those characters – common enough because they always push to the front – who promote themselves by denigrating the reputation of others. In attacking Burton he had more than enough supporters, for Burton had a gift for making enemies and even those who supported him scientifically, like David Livingstone, found him a blackguard. Burton's friends were other Disreputable Victorians like the flagellant poet Algernon Swinburne, the pornophile MP Monckton Milnes, and later on the decadent publisher (or publisher of decadent writers) Leonard Smithers.

They had some wild parties, but that wasn't quite what Burton's career needed.

Burton's life receded into a series of minor diplomatic posts enlivened by his own inimitable style: in the role of Her Majesty's Consul he presented the delighted King of Dahomey with pictures of nude white women. His reputation, both as a scholar and an outsider, was sealed with his translations of the *Arabian Nights*, the *Kama Sutra* and a version of *The Perfumed Garden*, which he translated from the French. Burton's discourses on the size of natives' penises and the various odours of pudenda met with less than universal approval.

Burton deserves this big book with its evidence of the hard work of real scholarship – Lovell's years spent deciphering and transcribing Burton's almost illegible hand and correcting the mistakes of earlier biographers. She comprehends, for example, that the silly, feminine diary which has previously been identified as Burton's own was in fact a spoof journal written by him as a satire on women travellers.

Lovell does not, however, fully understand the Burtons and pornography. She likes Burton, and wants to make him less of a bully, as she wants to make Isabel less of a prude, so she tries to reconcile the unreconcilable: Burton's writing of pornography with Isabel's burning it.

It was part of his domineering personality that Burton used his sexual explicitness to frighten others. His superiority in thus exciting shock and disgust gave him real pleasure. Isabel saw this as part of the self-destructive behaviour which she tried to curb in her husband. She saw only the damage which erotic work might do to his reputation, and recognised no value in his painstaking translation from rare Arabic manuscripts of *The Scented Garden* (so called to differentiate it from the earlier translation from the French). She therefore burned all manuscript copies of this and other erotic work shortly after his death. Lovell demonstrates that Isabel burned less of Burton's work than had previously been thought, but this is no defence for her actions. In the end, she betrayed the man she loved, making this book a tragedy as well as an adventure and love story.

Jad Adams

THREE

JUNGLES

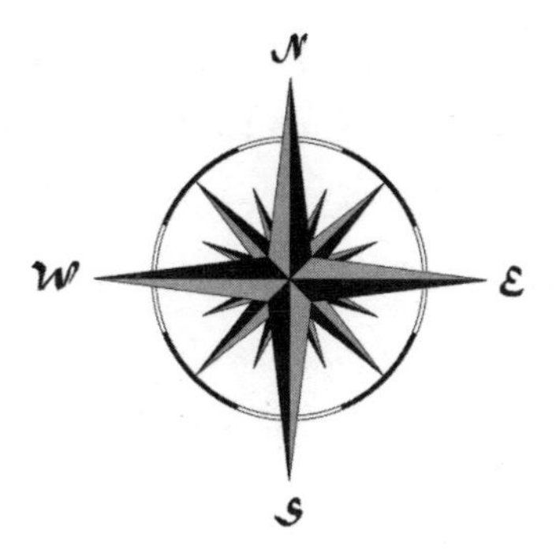

A city temple to rival Solomon's

Guardian, October 18 1864

Travels in the Central Parts of Indo-China (Siam), Cambodia, and Laos, during the years of 1858, 1859, and 1860 by the late M Henri Mouhot, French naturalist 2 vols. (John Murray, 1864).

A melancholy interest attaches to this beautiful book; beautiful as a specimen of typography, and as containing a perfect album of illustrations, of which it may be affirmed the like is seldom seen. The author, Henri Mouhot, fell a victim to jungle fever in the active prosecution of researches in the interior of Siam, a part of Asia unvisited by Europeans, but presenting those romantic but dangerous charms that attract the most ardent travellers.

M. Mouhot was a Frenchman, born at Montbéleard, in 1826. He was, therefore, under 40 at the date of his death, and, strange to say, had never known previous disease. Charmed by the fascinations of the virgin forests, where the tiger reigns supreme, the rhinoceros rolls his unwieldy frame, and the countless tribes of earth and air are actually fearless from ignorance of man, M. Mouhot, attended by two native servants, dived into their fearful depths, and braved the miasma of rank and putrid vegetation, the attacks of hordes of insects and crawling creatures which 'scent a man 20 feet off and hasten to suck his blood with a wonderful avidity,' and ran all the risks attendant upon wretched food, insufficient covering, and incessant exposure.

Perhaps the most important chapters of M. Mouhot's work have for their object the revelation of his discoveries at Nokhor or Angkor, the capital of the ancient kingdom of Cambodia or Khmer. In the province still bearing the name of Angkor, which is to the east of the great lake of Touli-sap, there are, on the banks of the Mekon, in the ancient kingdom of Tsiampois (Cochin China), ruins of the most surprising grandeur, extent, and artistic merit. 'One of these temples – a rival to that of Solomon, and erected by some ancient Michelangelo – might take an honourable place beside our most beautiful buildings. It is grander than anything left to us by Greece or Rome, and presents a sad contrast to the state of barbarism in which the nation is now plunged.' Time has crumbled many portions of these monuments; war, too, has injured them with its ruthless hoof, and the work of decay goes on beneath the all-devouring elements. But there stand memorials of a civilisation of the past worthy of the efforts of archaeologists and antiquaries; astounding in their extent, sublime in their beauty.

Who reared them? Who were the men that conceived, built, used them? They are attributed to a race of kings; as are the pyramids of Egypt. Did a slave population or a bond-people raise them? Many kings sat on the throne of Maha-Nocor-Khoner. 'There is a tradition of a leprous king, to whom is attributed the commencement of the great temple, but all else is forgotten. The inscriptions, with which some of the columns are covered, are illegible; and, if you interrogate the Cambodians as to the founders of the Angkor-Wat, you invariably receive one of these four replies: 'It is the work of Pra-Eun, the king of the angels;' 'It is the work of the giants;' 'It was built by a leprous king;' or else 'It made itself.' All these monuments, says M. Mouhot, were temples of Buddhism. But this is mere hypothesis, unsupported by his next statement, which assures us that the statues and bas-reliefs represent only secular subjects.

The slave trade and human sacrifices of Dahomey

Guardian, November 1 1864

A mission to Gelele, King of Dahome by Richard F Burton, late commissioner to Dahome, 2 vols. (Tinsley Brothers, 1864).

Dahomey is of all African kingdoms the best known by name to Europe, but there has been little real light thrown upon the facts of its history, civilisation, or condition. Many absurd notions have apparently spread in consequence of our ignorance of Dahomey and its people. Men generally well informed have given currency to extravagant ideas of their barbarity, and we have certainly laboured under considerable misapprehension of certain ferocious habits and customs supposed to be peculiar to the Dahomans. Indeed, our belief in some respects has been entirely based upon myth, but Captain Burton's pages go a long way in the process of correction. After all, he admits that Dahomey as it is exhibits a mixture of 'horrors and meanness,' a pitiless picture of mingled brutality and puerility, of 'ferocity and politeness.'

The attention of the British government has frequently been called to Dahomy. Captain Burton, however, brought the subject home to Earl Russell, by volunteering, in 1861, to visit Agbome. At that date it was not deemed advisable to accept this offer, but in 1863, while at Fernando Po, Captain Burton 'received the gratifying intelligence that Her Majesty's government had been pleased to choose him as the bearer of a friendly message to King Gelele.' Earl Russell's dispatch detailing the views of his colleagues lays stress upon the subject of the export of slaves from King Gelele's territories. The representative of this country is instructed to impress upon the king the importance which Her Majesty's government attaches to the cessation of this traffic. We learn from the document that Gelele had made a very sensible suggestion – viz. that white men should be prevented from coming to his dominions to buy slaves. Earl Russell promises to take steps to prevent their exportation, and alludes to the treaty with the United States, which will prevent, for the future, any American vessels coming to ship slaves.

When Captain Burton finally delivered the message in person to Gelele he obtained the following answer: 'That the slave trade was an ancestral custom, established by white men, to whom he would sell all they wanted – to the English, who, after greatly encouraging the export, had lately turned against it, palm oil and 'tree wool;' to the Portuguese, slaves. That a single article would not defray such expenses as those which I had witnessed.' It must be admitted, therefore, that the mission failed in obtaining a reduction in the export of slaves. The *argumentum ad hominem* was unpleasant enough, but to be told that Dahomey would still sell 'men and brothers' as common goods must have been disheartening in the extreme. 'Moreover,' the king added, 'the customs of his kingdom compelled him to make war, and that unless he sold he must slay his captives, which, England, perhaps, would like even less.' All that Captain Burton could do was to entreat to be heard in explanation before this reply was put on paper. He was heard, but the arguments urged did not prevent the transmission of the rejoinder as epitomised above.

The subject of human sacrifices was scarcely less satisfactorily dealt with. An influential journal has stated (July 4 1864,) that 'the King of Dahomey has lately been indulging in a sacrifice of 2,000 human beings simply in deference to a national prejudice, and to keep up the good old customs of the country. This turns out to be an exaggeration. The 'grand custom' of slaughter takes place on the death of the king, who, in the next world, is supposed to require soldiers, guards, attendants, servants, precisely as he does in the present. Such butchery is dreadful enough, but Captain Burton tells us that the 'annual' execution does not include more than eighty persons, chiefly criminals and prisoners of war. 'The executions,' says the captain, 'are, I believe, performed without cruelty.' Opinions, like tastes, differ, and we not only differ from the author, but convict him of self-contradiction. In his message he follows up his appeal against the sacrifices thus: 'It was, therefore, incumbent upon him [the King Gelele] to reduce the number of his sacrifices, and to spare his visitors the disgusting spectacle of nude and mutilated corpses hanging for two or three days in the sun; moreover, that, until such barbarities should be changed, I should advise all Englishmen who dislike 'tickling of the liver' (nausea), to avoid his court at customs' time.' The nude and mutilated corpses and the barbarity here mentioned can scarcely be separated from the universal ideas of cruelty.

There is a social institution which Captain Burton fully describes, of a peculiar and anomalous kind. We allude to the army of Amazons which constitutes an important portion of Gelele's army. Travellers' tales and 'long yarns' have represented the existence of immense bodies of these armed women. Captain Burton reduces their number to 2,000 at most. Of enormous size and strength, these females form an element of the population not to be despised. Their hideousness is equalled by their natural ferocity. And these giantesses are royal wives, jealously guarded from less than royal possession, no man being allowed to call one of them his own, at least such as are maidens. But nature is too powerful even for Dahoman law, and scandals of a delicate kind occur at Gelele's court. Captain Burton remarks that the king's progress was on one occasion delayed by the interesting condition of no less than 150 Amazons, who had taken to themselves paramours. But a difficulty of this kind is by no means insuperable in a court where woman reigns supreme. So complete is the acknowledgement of feminine influence that all offices are double. There are male and female ministers; two courts, masculine and feminine; each with its own privileges, rights, and immunities. The elucidation of these dual relationships is most curious; and the existence of an ideal 'mother' of men is the climax of this extraordinary arrangement. The late King of Dahomey is said to have placed great reliance on his Amazons; they were safeguards against treachery at home, and his best soldiers in general warfare. He ordered every father to bring his daughters to court, and of these the most likely were kept and trained to the use of weapons and armour. Of the Amazons now in Gelele's army, two thirds are said never to have been married, the remaining third having had husbands; and amongst them are to be found the bad-tempered of the sex, who are too troublesome for a quiet domestic life.

Hunting down the man-like ape of Borneo

Guardian, April 29 1869

The Malay Archipelago: the land of the Orang-utan, and the Bird of Paradise, by Alfred Russel Wallace, 2 vols. (Macmillan and Co. 1869).

Nature has been said by someone to delight in contrasts, and certainly no more striking contrast can be suggested than that of the title of these volumes *The Land of the OrangUutan and the Bird of Paradise*, bipeds, as everybody knows, of most opposite externals and characteristics. The land in which one of the ugliest of mammals and one of the most beautiful of birds exist in the same forests has long continued to be one of the least known to Europeans, and we do not hesitate to say that to the late intrepid and untiring Rajah Brooke we are mainly indebted for what information travellers are permitted to gather and lay before us. Of these Eastern travellers,

Mr Russel Wallace may be classed amongst the most thoughtful, as he proves himself to have been one of the most successful, of naturalists.

He was eight years in the Indian archipelago of the Pacific. He went there as a cultured scientific observer. He had a worthy object in view, and had prepared for its prosecution and accomplishment; and after diligently pursuing that object, he returned to England in 1862, to find himself 'surrounded by a room full of packing-cases, containing the collections that I had from time to time sent home for my private use. These comprised nearly three thousand bird skins, of about a thousand species; besides some quadrupeds and shells.' A perfect museum of tropical natural history in the Pacific, and a quite sufficient explanation of the six years' delay which has occurred in the publication of his book. Of this book as a contribution to natural science and history we cannot speak too highly. It is full of fresh facts, and it is excellently written.

As a contributor of new facts for Mr Charles Darwin, he has also been exceedingly prolific. The interesting questions of species and organic development have doubtless received from Mr Wallace no inconsiderable service, and the great prophet of the development theory cannot but be very thankful for such able and enthusiastic disciples as the author of the *Malay Archipelago*. At the same time we seem to become conscious, as we read, of a growing conviction that the Darwinians are students with monocular vision only – very clear, very safe, very deep vision of its kind, but wanting the natural complement and correction of a double-eyed power. However, as Mr Wallace does not pretend to discuss the principles of the theory he desires to support, but aims only at affording correct information and exciting a true scientific love for his favourite studies, we shall say nothing of the Darwinian notion, but help him, as far as our space will permit, to the worthy object he has in view:

'One of my chief objects in coming to stay at Simunjon was to see the orang-utan (or great man-like ape of Borneo) in his native haunts, to study his habits, and obtain good specimens of the different varieties and species of both sexes, and of the adult and young animals. In all these objects I succeeded beyond my expectations…

'… It is a singular and very interesting sight to watch an orangutan or 'mias' as it is called by the natives, making his way leisurely through the forest. He walks deliberately along some of the larger branches, in the semi-erect attitude which the great length of his arms and the shortness of his legs cause him naturally to assume; and the disproportion between these limbs is increased by his walking on his knuckles, not on the palm of the hand, as we should do. He seems always to choose those branches which intermingle with an adjoining tree, on approaching which he stretches out his long arms, and, seizing the opposing boughs, grasps them together with both hands, seems to try their strength, and then deliberately swings himself across to the next branch, on which he walks along as before. He never jumps or springs, or even appears to hurry himself, and yet manages to get along almost as quickly as a person can run through the forest beneath.

'The long and powerful arms are of the greatest use to the animal, enabling it to climb easily up the loftiest trees, to seize fruits and young leaves from slender boughs which will not bear its weight, and to gather leaves and branches with which to form its nest … This is placed low down, however, on a small tree not more than 20ft to 50ft from the ground, probably because it is warmer and less exposed to wind than higher up. Each mias is said to make a fresh one for himself every night; but I should think that is hardly probable, or their remains would be much more abundant; for though I saw several about the coal mines, there must have been many orangs about every day, and in a year their deserted nests would become very numerous. The Dyaks say that, when it is very wet, the mias covers himself over with leaves of pandanus, or large ferns, which has perhaps led to the story of his making a hut in the trees. The orang does not leave his bed till the sun has well risen and dried up the dew upon the leaves. He feeds all through the middle of the day, but seldom returns to the same tree two days running. They do not seem much alarmed at man, as they often stared down upon me for several minutes, and then only moved away slowly to an adjacent tree …'

'Dr Livingstone, I presume?'

Guardian, July 4 1872

On January 23 1871, Mr Stanley, special commissioner of the *New York Herald*, who had left Zanzibar at the head of a large caravan organised by himself, reached Unyanyembe, having lost by sickness on the way one of the white men who had started out with him, two of his armed escort, eight pagazis, two horses, and 27 asses. Resting here for a few days, he prepared to carry out his determination of proceeding to Ujiji, when to his annoyance, he found that Mirambo, the King of Ujowa, had, in some fit of alarm or other at the incursion which had been made

A jungle explorer

into his territory, announced that in future no caravan should pass to Ujiji over the land owned by him, unless it went over his dead body.

The Arabs, incensed at this curtailment of their rights, had declared war against Mirambo; and as they appeared to be confident of victory and determined to fight well, Mr Stanley judged that the better course was for him to combine with them in attacking the King of Ujowa. Accordingly he joined his forces, and the united strength advanced into the enemy's territory. The first day was succesful for the Arabs, who succeeded in surprising three of Mirambo's villages, and captured, killed, or drove away the inhabitants. On the second day of the warlike expedition Mr Stanley caught a fever, and was reconveyed to Unyanyembe. The third day an Arab detachment incautiously attacked another of the Ujowa villages, and were at first victorious; but Mirambo, who was commanding his men in person, gradually drew the Arabs into an ambush, and then defeated them with great slaughter, killing 17 of their chieftains, and also five of the armed men who belonged to Mr Stanley's expedition.

This mishap appears to have thoroughly disheartened the Arabs, for on the fourth day of hostilites they deserted in every direction, at the same time carrying panic among the men who formed Mr Stanley's force, so effectually that they too made the best of their way to the coast, leaving the American traveller with only an Englishman, named Shaw, an Arab boy called Selim, and six of the armed escort. Apprehensions having then arisen that if news of the break-up of his enemy's forces should reach Mirambo that potentate would immediately make preparations for attacking Unyanyembe itself, Mr Stanley, who had by this time somewhat recovered from his fever, collected all the fugitives he could find, and, having succeeded in organising about 150 of them into a tolerably compact band, and obtaining five days' provisions for them, barricaded a number of houses, hoisted the American flag, and awaited Mirambo's approach. The King of Ujowa, however, left Unyanyembe unmolested.

It now occurred to Mr Stanley that the better course to pursue would be to leave the Arabs to fight out their own battles, and attempt to reach Ujiji by a more northerly route – the more so because he saw no prospect of any speedy conclusion to the war which had begun between Arabs and Mirambo. To this the Arabs offered serious objection, doubtless from selfish motives, and, failing to dissuade Mr Stanley, they did their best to intimidate his followers by means of extraordinary tales. In this endeavour they were so far successful that Shaw, the Englishman, after proceeding a part of the journey, declined to go further, and it was with great difficulty that the American could obtain bearers for his baggage or an escort.

At last, however, he started, and, entering the desert, passed through several hundred miles of country scarcely known to the Arabs themselves.

Several times he was so seriously threatened by the rapacious chiefs of hostile tribes that he had the greatest difficulty in proceeding; it was only by cajolling here and by threatening there that he was able to escape their attempted extortions and delays. On the November 3 1871, he came in sight of the outlying houses of Ujiji, and, anxious to enter the African town with as much éclat as possible, he disposed his little band in such a manner as to form a somewhat imposing procession. At the head was borne the American flag; next came the armed escort, who were directed to discharge their firearms with as much rapidity as possible; following these were the baggage men, the horses, and the asses; and in the rear of all came Mr Stanley himself. The din of the firing aroused the inhabitants of Ujiji to the fact that strangers were approaching, and they flocked out in great crowds, filling the air with deafening shouts and beating violently on their rude musical instruments.

As the procession entered the town Mr Stanley observed a group of Arabs on the right, in the centre of whom was a pale-looking bearded white man, whose fair skin contrasted with the sunburnt visages of those by whom he was surrounded. Passing from the rear of the procession to the front, the American traveller noticed the white man was clad in a red woollen jacket, and wore upon his head a naval cap with a faded gilt band round it. In an instant he recognised the European as none other than Dr Livingstone himself; and he was about to rush forward and embrace him, when the thought occurred that he was in the presence of Arabs, who, being accustomed to conceal their feelings, were very likely to found their estimate of a man upon the manner in which he conceals his own. A dignified Arab chieftain, moreover, stood by, and this confirmed Mr Stanley in his resolution to show no symptom of rejoicing or excitement. Slowly advancing towards the great traveller, he bowed and said, 'Dr Livingstone, I presume?' To which address the latter, who was fully equal to the occasion, simply smiled and replied 'Yes.' It was not till some hours afterwards, when alone together, seated on a goatskin, that the two white men exchanged those congratulations which both were eager to express, and recounted their respective difficulties and adventures.

Mr Stanley's statement is that Dr Livingstone appeared to be in remarkably good health, stout, and strong, quite undismayed by all that he had gone through, and eager only to finish the task he had imposed upon himself. The doctor having been shut out from the civilised world for so many years, Mr Stanley found himself acting as a kind of newspaper to him, and the details of what had occurred in Europe and America interested him exceedingly.

Dr Livingstone's story of his adventures was to the following effect. In March 1866, he started from Zanzibar. The expedition which he led consisted of 12 sepoys, nine Johanna men, seven liberated slaves, and two Zambesi men – in all 30 persons. At first Dr Livingstone travelled along the left bank of the Rovuma River; but as he pursued his way, his men began to grow disaffected and frightened; and, in spite of all his efforts to manage and keep them together, most of them left him and returned to their homes, spreading everywhere the report of his death as a reason for their re-appearance there.

In August, 1866, he arrived in the territory of Mponda, a chief who rules over a tribe living near the N'yassa Lake; and here Wikoteni, a protege of the doctor's, insisted upon being absolved from going any further. After resting for a short time in Mponda's ground, Dr Livingstone proceeded to inspect the 'heel' of the N'yassa Lake; and it was while carrying out this enterprise that the Johanna men, who had till now remained faithful, deserted him, alleging as their excuse that a chief named Mazitu had suddenly taken to plundering, and was ill-using travellers who ventured into his neighbourhood. It is probable that the doctor would not have lost the services of those men had their leader been a man of more decided character; but Musa – for that was his name – appeared to be more frightened than his subordinates, and when he deserted they fled also. To account for their conduct, they also invented a story of Dr Livingstone's death, and their mendacious tales were the foundation of the reports which – though fairly exploded some years ago – have circulated more or less ever since.

In December, 1866, Dr Livingstone decided upon advancing in a northerly direction. Approaching King Cazembe's territory, he crossed a thin stream called the Chambezi; and here he found himself in great difficulty, being for a long while unable to discover to what the river belonged. The confusion which he experienced was greatly increased by the fact that Portuguese travellers had previously reported the existence of such a stream, and has asserted that it was a tributary of the great Zambezi River, having no connection whatever with the Nile. From the beginning of 1867 to the middle of March, 1869, he traversed the banks of the mysterious stream, tracing where it ran, and proving conclusively that Chambezi was not the head of the Zambezi. He established conclusively (first) that the Portuguese Zambezi and the Chambezi are totatally distinct streams; and (second) that the Chambezi is the head waters for the Nile.

He followed the course of the Chambezi for several hundred miles and had come within 180 miles of that part of the Nile which has already been traced, when the men he had with him mutinied and deserted him. Having now neither stores nor followers, he was obliged to retire to Ujiji, weary and destitute. It was soon after this that Mr Stanley found him.

TP O'Connor

Miss Mary Kingsley and her African explorations

Guardian, March 20 1896

A meeting of the Liverpool Geographical Society was held last night, when a paper by Miss Mary Kingsley upon her recent explorations in West Africa was read by Mr J Irvine, Miss Kingsley being present.

Miss Kingsley stated that her object in going to West Africa was to make a collection of fishes from a river north of the Congo, and also to study the subject of native law and culture. After spending some months in Old Calabar River, she proceeded to the French Congo, and went up the Ogowe River, and from thence to the river Rembwe. Much of the journey was accomplished on foot, and during her march she had some very rough experiences. On one occasion she arrived wearing an astrakhan-like collar of leeches, a complete over-cloak of mud, streaked with blood and bespangled with flies, having been wading up to her neck in the swamp.

From the Rembwe River she proceeded to Corsico Island, thence to the foot of the Cameroons Peak, the description of the ascent of which formed the leading part of her paper. She stated that the delta region was intensely interesting both in its flora, fauna and fetish. It was called Kara Country, and its main population consisted of malaria microbes and mosquitoes, and it was supremely damp. Of the Fan tribes she formed a very high opinion, speaking of them as a brave, athletic, and well-formed race.

She left Victoria, at the base of the Cameroons mountain, in fine weather, and speaking of the new road which the German government is making, she described it as the most magnificent, both in breadth and general intention that she had ever seen in Africa. It ran through a 'superbly beautiful' country, and on either side there was a deep drain to carry off the surface water. Having described the beauties of the scenery and vegetation, Miss Kingsley and her band of carriers encountered two terrific thunderstorms, in which the lightning was to be seen running about the ground like water. The peak was reached after four days' travelling, and after becoming engrossed with the splendour of the view to be obtained from the top, Miss Kingsley suddenly became aware that her carriers had departed. She 'scuttled' down the side of the mountain and plunged into the wall of mist rising up its sides, and succeeded in finding one of her natives named Zenia, in regard to whom she had been warned that he was slightly crazy. This, she said, was a bad position for a fine lady, to be left with lunatic, and no outfit save an empty lantern and the lid of a saucepan, which he had thoughtfully brought with him for a load.

Miss Kingsley found in the cairn on the summit of the mountain that some predecessor had put all the notices left by others, from Sir Richard Burton onwards into a tin box. Referring to the trade possibilities of West Africa, Miss Kingsley made an earnest appeal to Englishmen to extend the empire in those parts, pointing out the value of their position as markets for English manufactures, especially in view of the fact that other West African districts under German and French control were closed against us by high preferential tariffs. If the hinterland was not kept open we would speedily lose what generations of enterprise had secured for the English nation.

As to the unhealthiness of the climate, she observed that, whereas the holding of our West African markets drains a few hundred men only too often forever, the trade they carried on and developed enables thousands of men, women, and children to remain safe in England in comfort and pleasure, owing to the wages and profits arising from maunfactures and exports. She trusted that those at home would give all honour to men who were still working in West Africa, and to the memory of those lying buried in the weed-grown, snake infested cemeteries and the pathless swamps of the coast.

She hoped England might never dream of forfeiting or playing with the conquests won for her by heroes of commerce whose battles had been fought on lonely beaches far from home, in contest with the foe only to be seen in the dreams of delirium, which takes the form of a poison in aching brains and burning veins, namely the dread west coast fever.

Mrs Isabella Bishop: A Famous Traveller

Guardian, October 11 1904

The death of Mrs Isabella Bishop has taken place at Edinburgh. She had been ill for many months, and her strength had failed gradually. Isabella Bird – who by her marriage became Mrs Bishop – was undoubtedly the foremost woman traveller of our time. Her wanderings, only a small portion of which are recorded in her nine published works, included the United States, the Hawaii Islands, Australia, New Zealand, Japan, Korea, China, India, Lesser Tibet, Malacca, Persia and Kurdistan, Syria, Armenia and Morocco. Mrs Bishop was equally at home in them all. She possessed the true traveller's faculty of disregarding inconveniences and extracting all possible enjoyment from the moment. Recalling her disgust at the first night's quarters in western China, she remarks: 'Many a hearty meal and ten hours' sleep I afterwards came to enjoy in dens which at first seemed foul and hopeless.' The elation of leaving civilization behind proved sufficient at any time to compensate her for all disagreeables. Though giving her readers to understand that her health was far from robust, Mrs Bishop generally contributed to knock up her escort, whether native or European, remaining herself in excellent condition. While crossing the mountains of Persia in severe weather nearly all her men were on the sick list, but it was not until the last march, a long but comparatively easy ride into Teheran, that Mrs Bishop herself gave in, arriving at the residence of the British ambassador speechless and only half conscious.

Isabella Bird was the daughter of a rector of Tattenhall in Cheshire and was born in 1832. Her first experience of traveling was gained in 1855 when she visited the United States with some relations, her experiences being recounted anonymously in *An Englishwoman in America*, which appeared in 1857. Some years later, Miss Bird visited Australia and New Zealand for her heath, and was detained by accident at Hawaii. Here she began to adopt unconventional modes of travelling, learned to ride astride, Hawaii fashion, spent a night in a native village, and twice climbed to the crater of Mauna Loa. *Six Months in the Sandwich Islands* gave a readable account of her visit. The passion for travel had now fairly seized Miss Bird. She spent the following winter (1873) in the Rocky mountains, riding 800 miles through snow and rocky defiles, living for the most part in a log hut with a skunk's lair beneath. For many weeks Miss Bird was the only woman among the snow-bound squatters and hunters of Estes Park, but there, as everywhere throughout the west, she met with unvarying courtesy and deference. In 1878 Miss Bird spent some months in Japan, traversing the island of Hondo from Tokyo to its northerly extremity, and crossing to Yezo where she paid a visit to the 'hairy Ainos'. Her only companion was a native boy, Ito, and she lived on Japanese food (rice, eggs, and a fowl when Ito could catch one) and slept in native inns. Much of the country was unvisited by Europeans, but beyond the wearying curiosity of the Japanese she met with no annoyance. Her two volumes, *Unbeaten tracks in Japan* are delightful reading, full of charming descriptive touches. They may be said to have introduced the reading public at home to, at any rate, the superficial fascination of Japan. She criticised severely the unsympathetic attitude of the ordinary European missionary to native ideas and beliefs, and though an ardent believer in missions, which she aided by several medical foundations in the East, yet here, as elsewhere, she unsparingly exposed defects in their methods of working. On her way home Miss Bird paid a flying visit to the native States of the Malay Peninsula, and drew a vivid picture of their flower-tangled jungles in *The Golden Chersonese*, which appeared in 1882. The ravages of mosquitos, though extremely severe upon this occasion, could not destroy her pleasure or dull the quickness of eye or pen.

In 1881 Miss Bird became the wife of Dr John Bishop, who, however, died in 1886. His widow at once recommenced travelling. A tour in Syria and Palestine was followed by a severe winter journey to Teheran, which is described with much spirit in her next book, *Journeys in Persia and Kurdistan*, published in 1891. In some respects this is the best of her works, for both country and people are full of interest and variety, and her journey included a visit to some of the little-known Christian settlements in Syria, whose archaic ceremonies and curious way of living she sympathetically describes. The winter journey across the mountains from Bagdad to Teheran entailed extreme hardships. At the end of one day's march, during which another party was found frozen to death on the way, the night was passed in a room where no fire could be lit and where 'the wall was full of cracks big enough for a finger, through which the night wind rioted in a temperature five degrees below zero.' Frequently the best lodging available was a stable, the travellers camping in a dark recess among horses and mules. On her return journey from Teheran Mrs Bishop passed through a disturbed Bakhtiari district and once at least her party was under fire. In Syria a fresh danger arose, for north of Lake Urini the Kurds perpetually raided the villages, and incessant watchfulness was necessary. In spite of the utmost care, she lost many valuables, her chief camp comforts, and her journals. Nothing could exceed the misery of the picture drawn by Mrs Bishop of the Armenian villages, continually harried by Kurds, who were nothing less than authorised robbers. The account of the Armenian community at Kochanes, the headquarters of the patriarch, is extremely interesting in its mingling of wretched poverty, quaint ecclesiastical forms and absolute devotion to a persecuted religion.

The Far East next engaged Mrs Bishop's attention. Several years were spent almost entirely in Asia. From India and Kashmir she penetrated into Little Tibet, recounting her experiences in a small, brightly written volume entitled *Among the Thibetans*. In crossing a flooded river Mrs Bishop's horse rolled over; she was nearly drowned but escaped with a broken rib, which, however, only delayed her journey for a day. Korea and China were next explored. The chief interest of *Corea and her Neighbours* is political, for Mrs Bishop's visit was interrupted by the Japanese invasion, and she saw something of what went on behind the scenes. The account of her journey through the Chinese province of Szechuan, embodied in two stout volumes, *The Yangtze Valley and Beyond*, is more attractive to the general reader, and is fully illustrated from Mrs Bishop's photographs. She ascended the Yangtse in a native 'wupan,' or houseboat, crossed the plain of Chengtu in an open chair, travelled through the mountainous western district of the province, and penetrated even beyond the Chinese border. Here she found a subjugated tribe, the Mantse, with a European type of feature and architecture and customs differing widely from those of the Mongolian races.

The land travelling was extremely rough, and the inns were filthy. The mountain scenery, however, was magnificent – Alpine peaks with sub-tropical vegetation beneath – and made up, in the traveller's opinion, for all discomforts. In the small villages the people were generally friendly, but in the towns her open chair roused native fanaticism, and twice she was violently attacked. Though her journey was not interrupted, it was long before she fully recovered from a blow received in one of these assaults. Apart form their fanaticism Mrs Bishop thought well of the Chinese, as a race of great vigour and many good qualities. Without taking an extreme view of the opium question, she considered that opium smoking was sapping the strength of the race. Almost all her bearers and attendants had contracted the habit and were liable to be incapacitated at any time.

A lover of Africa

Observer, October 9 1910

A Voice from the Congo, Comprising Stories, Anecdotes and Descriptive Notes, by Herbert Ward (Heinemann, 10s)

There are many ways of looking at Africa; and Mr Ward and his old chief, Stanley, looked at it with different eyes. Stanley loved its infinite possibilities of adventure, its mystery and provocation, its sense of tremendous obstacles to be overcome, but he did not love it for its own sake. That is just what Mr Ward does. He might be the hero of his own story of the man who, sailing for Europe after 20 years of life in Africa, exclaimed on reaching San Thome: 'I want to go back. I've had enough of Europe.' It is something like the love of children. Some people love children, not because they are pretty, or amusing, or good, but because they are children. And Mr Ward likes Africans – children, too, in their way – full knowing the worst of them, and has to apologise for their abominations on the ground of their 'imperfect evolution' and their 'never having had a chance.' Both counts are true. Africa represents primitive barbarism in a world which is otherwise comparatively civilised, but not civilised enough to be merciful to the weak. Cruelty, superstition, cannibalism are the phenomena of the childhood of all races; and, after all, the horrors which Africa practises on herself are no worse than the horrors which Europe and America have practised on her. There is not much to choose between the native witch-doctor and the late King Leopold.

One looks, first of all, for what Mr Ward has to say of Stanley, with whose march across the continent he was so closely associated. 'Personally,' he says, 'Stanley impressed me as a man whose life had been embittered, and he appeared to take it as an accepted fact that every man's hand was against him.' Ward once told him he had the reputation of being hard. 'Hard!' said Stanley. 'You've got to be hard. If you're not hard, you're weak. There are only two sides to it.' 'My dear fellow,' he said to Ward on another occasion, 'in this world we can't stop to think about the impressions we create – no time for that sort of thing.'

Somehow Livingstone managed to get along without being 'hard.' Ward had an account of his death from an old native who was with him during the later years:

'Dr Livingstone was an old man?'

'Ah, yes, very old; he had no teeth, but they boiled his meat soft.'

'What did Dr Livingstone say to you all when you arrived with Stanley at Ujiji?'

'He said: "I am very happy, you have brought me my child." Ah, he was a good old man, and we called him "Bwana Makubwa." Stanley told us he was a great man.'

'Did the people all like him?'

'Oh, master, they loved him very much.'

'Tell me about his death.'

'Well: the Bwana Makubwa was sick about six days in a hut in the middle of the village Kataui, on the shores of the Lake Bemba. He used to put his hand on his chest and say that there the pain was. He died at sundown, but just before that he gave us some papers and told us to take them to the consul at Zanzibar, and also his big dog. When he was dead we all cried, and the natives also.'

Mr Ward's own relations with the natives seem to have resembled those of Livingstone rather than Stanley. At all events, he had no difficulty in getting on good terms with them. Mr Ward was present at an execution for murder. In the centre of the market place the culprit, Lubaki, had been buried in a hole, from which his head was alone visible. 'The village executioner, a muscular native, was bidden forward by the chief. He carried in his arms a large rock, weighing at least a hundredweight. At a given word, the great stone fell upon Lubaki's head.'

It is in central Africa that cannibalism is to be seen at its worst. The thing is an organised trade: there are regular markets for the sale of human beings for purposes of food. In some cases they are deliberately fattened; and among some of the riverside tribes of the Upper Congo the belief prevails that 'the flavour of human flesh is improved by submerging the prospective victim up to the neck in the water for two or three days previous to sacrifice'.

Probably the most inhuman practice of all is to be met with among the tribes who deliberately hawk the victim piecemeal whilst still alive.

Incredible as it may appear, the treatment remains justified by abundant proof, as well as from personal observation, that captives were led from place to place in order that individuals might have the opportunity of indicating, by external marks on the body, the portion they desired to acquire. The distinguishing marks were generally made by means of coloured clay or strips of grass tied in a peculiar fashion.

Mr Ward's is not in any sense a formal study of Congo conditions, but a series of sketches and jottings embodying his own observations and experiences. It takes us nearer the heart of the problem than many more pretentious volumes; and its sympathy and humanity will commend it to a wide circle of readers.

Penelope is travelling

Guardian, August 4 1925

New York City: Penelope is travelling. She is not only buying out the Galerie Lafayette lock, stock, and barrel. She is going farther and doing worse. She is making 'the last outposts of romance' as real and familiar as the kitchen sink. Little Mme David returns to Paris from Main Street, Lhassa, Tibet, where she has been living quiet. What she has to say about the drove of gentlemen who have been advertising themselves as the first and only visitor to Lhassa is mostly smile. Othello used to be the life of the party. Now we have Clare Sheridan and Bessie Beatty reciting hair-breadth escapes midst field and flood and lonely journeys beyond forbidden frontiers to tired business men and chair-ridden editors.

The International Association of Woman Explorers has been founded. The charter members of the American branch have sent out invitations to the English, Danish, French, and German woman travellers of renown, inviting them to form their own national chapters. The nucleus of the American members is Harriet Chalmers Adams, FRGS, who has followed the trail of the conquistadors all over Spain, Mexico, and South America; Jean Kenyon Mackensie, who was for years a missionary in the Cameroons and who has not only written *Black Sheep* and two other charming books about life in the jungle forest of Africa but has made notable anthropological records on language and taboo; Gertrude Emerson, one of the editors of 'Asia,' who has travelled by herself in Indo-China, India, and the Philippines, and who was one of the first American women to cross by sanipan the submerged forest that lies on the road to Angkor, lost city of the Khmer kings in Cambodia; Marguerite Harrison, who laughs at prisons, makes adventurous journeys to Sakalin and last year took the 300 mile trek with the Bakhtiari tribe through the mountains of Western Persia and collaborated in taking the motion-picture *Grass*; Marv Austin, authority on Indian life in the south-west; Rose Wilder Lane, whose 'Peaks of Shala' records her journey into the mountain valleys of Albania; Blair Niles and Gertrude Matthews Shelby, both of whom have records as explorers in South America.

A good crowd and a crowd with a sense of humour. You can see that they have had many a hearty laugh at the expense of 'The Circumnavigators' and other organisations of men who drink toasts to whoever is just back from the Pole, swap yarns about Shanghai and Capetown, or eat the regular lunch and call it tiffin.

The International Association of Woman Explorers avow no purpose – but to have a banquet. They propose to have an annual feast in honour of the principal woman explorer of the year. They would hale Mme David over from Paris this autumn if they could. Blair Niles, I suppose, will make a speech about how the men explorers are not to write their books in Munchausen ink. She has never forgiven one gentleman for the unreachable romantic wildness of his book on Mongolia. She thinks it isn't fair for people with the fiction touch to write travel-books. It makes life too hard for an honest woman who only puts down what she sees with her eyes open. That whole subject is a thing that has to be considered now that Penelope is travelling. Take the South Sea Islands, for instance. Some pretty tall and lustrous stories used to be told by Ulysses and O'Brien about the luring damsels of Tahiti. My theory is that with his sisters, cousins, and aunts taking all the steamers to coral strands the gentleman explorer will simply not find the hula-hula dance as beautiful as once he did.

This makes for another problem, a very special problem for women explorers armed with typewriters and fountain-pens, coming late to the scene. The tradition of the traveller and of his bible is Romance. And Romance being what it is, won't Desdemona have to go in for something else to stand her in good stead when returning to the annual banquet and to Othello! Fortunately, there is science. The women explorers hope to return not only with competent 'copy' about life and customs in remote places, but with substantial scientific data.

I asked one of the founders if the banquet was really all. She said she supposed one or two of them would meet and exchange yarns now and

that it tallied exactly with native rumours that the Indians believed that Fawcett never wanted to reach home again.'

A gentleman in the jungle

Observer, December 16 1962

The Albert N'Yanza by Sir Samuel Baker (Sidgwick & Jackson, 2 vols, £4 4s)

The British Empire was not acquired in a fit of absence of mind. It was got in decades of surety of self. The Victorians were so certain they were right that even their enemies suspected they might be. And the rightest of them all was Sir Samuel Baker. In the 1860s, the discovery of the source of the Nile was the lure of explorers. Where Caesar had failed the English gentleman should succeed. First Burton and then Speke and Grant struck out from Zanzibar. Burton returned, his successors vanished. The wealthy Mr and Mrs Baker, on a shooting trip in the Sudan, were asked to find them.

Samuel Baker was a thorough man. Wherever he went, his predjudices and paraphernalia went, too. Only Baker could have a sponge bath carried round central Africa for two years and produce a clean kilt, sporran and Glengarry bonnet to overawe an African chieftain several thousand miles from Perth. He was forewarned and forearmed to the teeth, never was explorer better prepared. Fate squealed for mercy when Baker came into view.

The Bakers set out from Khartoum and found Speke and Grant, who had unfortunately already discovered the source of the Nile. Baker was disappointed and asked if one leaf of the laurel remained for him. The successful explorers gave him a map, and said that there was still a great lake to be explored on the upper reaches of the Nile. The Bakers immediately decided to map this lake for the honour of England and the Royal Geographical Society.

The Albert N'Yanza describes the story of the Bakers' round trip over two years to the unknown lake, which Baker names as an 'imperishable memorial' to the Prince Consort, a man 'loved and mourned by our gracious Queen and deplored by every Englishman.' Imperturbably, the Bakers outwit slave traders, cataracts, sunstroke, hippopotami, fever, and vermilion-coloured savages twanging at them with poisoned arrows. Baker himself slaughters every bit of formidable fauna and notes or eats every bit of fancy flora. He is crass in action, yet acute in description. He is a caricature of the sporting gentleman, yet a genius of competence. He has the answer for everything, from defeating a swordsman by ramming his umbrella down his opponents throat to using fish skins to bind the butts of rifles. With fist, bullet or stiff upper lip, he outfaces every situation: his wife is as doughty. He gives her his ultimate praise. She was, he tells us, 'no *screamer*.'

Baker's prose is unexpected. It is dry, exact, and ironic. He is a joy to read, especially in this edition, which is a printer's triumph. His judgments of Africa are brutal and patronising; but even though he thinks the African natives are inferior in nature to the noble dog, he concedes that, given the appalling conditions of life, they probably behave better than Europeans would. They have, indeed, to be forced to witness public executions, which European ladies flock to see.

Once, and only once, Baker even laughs at himself. He has ordered his men to give three cheers for England and the sources of the Nile. They do, and Baker notices that the hurrahs must be to them a wild, and even savage, yell. It was through such a small chink in the armour of self-righteousness that the English began to feel guilty of their patronage and to set an Empire free.

Andrew Sinclair

A walk in the crocodile's shoes

Guardian, February 9 2002

Explorers who make a living by writing about their expeditions know that it takes two journeys to make a book: the physical slog is followed by its recreation in literary form. And the second can be even more perilous than the first. Benedict Allen wasn't quite as green as the rainforest when he decided, at 22, to beat a path alone from the Orinoco to the Amazon. After all, he'd got a BSc in environmental science, and a doctorate in self-possession. But by the time the flora and fauna and the ethnic tribes were through with him, he also had dysentery and malaria, and depression and doubt in double doses.

But it was the tribe he wanted to join back home that gave him the toughest time of all. 'Too big for his jungle boots,' huffed worthies at the Royal Geographical Society, at 1 Kensington Gore, SW7. Maybe they didn't like the first whiff of young Allen they got from a tale in a tabloid paper of how, starving, he ate his dog – kidneys and liver first. Or perhaps it was that the title of his book – *Mad White Giant* – was gung-ho, when it should have been more respectful of the Victorian tradition of exploring that they assumed was his model. It didn't occur to some of the pith-heads at the RGS that Allen might have been mocking himself – there are over two gangly yards of him, and his clumsiness through the trip-root, creeper-noosed foliage made him the despair of his shoeless guides, who were fleeter than people wearing Air Jordans.

'I appeared from nowhere, having done this big journey as someone nobody really knew,' he reflects, almost 20 years on, in his eyrie in Shepherd's Bush. 'I had been in the *Daily Mail* as the man who ate his dog to survive. They didn't like the whole Indiana Jones element, I was an adventurer, an upstart. But it's the unfairness with which they judged, and prejudged, that hurt.'

There was a spat about authenticity with Dr James Hemming, director of the RGS, whose portals he didn't darken for a while – but one of whose pillars he has now become. 'I was seething,' he says. So much so that his mother feared he would stomp off on a dangerously challenging trip, just to prove his critics wrong. Even now, with a cache of books and TV series chronicling his lone adventuring, from voodoo in Haiti to crocodile cults in New Guinea, it rankles with Allen to be reminded that some didn't believe he had covered so much terrain so quickly by foot and by canoe.

So much so that the author's note in the first edition (1985) that says, 'I have been at pains to omit more than fleeting anthropological, ecological and geographical references', is supplemented in the new paperback with a warning to pedantic readers that if 'cultural and geographical blunders scream out at you', remember this was a young guy 'launching out into an exotic world which he didn't, and couldn't understand'. Allen says that, even on that trip, he realised that what would be required back home, if he was to be accepted by the experts, would be a 'careful, detailed record of such a fiendishly long trek'.

He admits now that he was naive; that he was 'messed up' by the hardships. But he wasn't the romantic soul some made him out to be. From the first, he set a goal for his exploration and scrupulously made notes (and comic doodles), but some on that venture were lost when his canoe was capsized by the dog which became several dinners.

Early on, too, he began to build the idea of a different kind of adventuring: 'It was a bit naive, but I thought that if the locals don't need money, and I could lock into their system, I wouldn't be held back by the problems of trying to keep in contact with the outside world. I'd also be free from the mental baggage.

'All [my] expeditions became a bid to leave as much of the west behind as possible.' Unlike other equipment-laden explorers, he, a solo voyager, had the chance to glimpse obscure cults and customs. 'To me, it's a question of going back to people who've been bypassed and entering their world.' In New Guinea, he says he sought out members of a tribal crocodile cult who eventually permitted him to take part in their initiation rites [described in *Into the Crocodile's Nest*]. In spite of contact with the outside world, the tribe keeps up the ceremony, but now its usefulness to them is 'as a map of the mind. It's how they use the crocodile as a role model in the forest.'

Each remote little community, he says, offers a 'little window in how to see and interpret life and I am trying to get through that window.' But he'd stumbled on something else, too, although he didn't realise it till he began writing *Mad White Giant* back home – a new subgenre of travel writing. Bruce Chatwin had discovered (or rediscovered) it, by adding an imaginative component to his journeys but Allen says his tales from the tangled woods are to be read as poetic accounts of what happened to him. There's a lot of personal information in that first book.

Now, 'pretty well all the great physical journeys have been done' by someone or other. But Allen is still outward-bound, and less than half as old as Wilfred Thesiger. 'Now is an era of idea,' he says, so though his next book will be about the Amazon, it won't be a conventional account of it as an eco-system, a green hell, or a paradise, but as a fabulous river of the imagination. 'I'd like to work out what it really is: maybe it's an unanswerable question; maybe it's a little bit of everyone.'

John Cunningham

Veil lifts on jungle mystery of the vanishing colonel

Observer, March 21 2004

It is an unsolved riddle which has inspired explorers and writers for nearly 80 years. Yet now, after a decade of research, one British writer and director has shed unexpected light on the murky fate of Colonel Percy Harrison Fawcett and those who followed him deep into the Brazilian jungle. It has long been assumed that the missing colonel, a celebrated explorer who knew the popular adventure writers Rider Haggard and Arthur Conan Doyle, must have been murdered by Amazonian tribesmen in 1925 during his fabled expedition to find the Lost City of Z. The truth, however, turns out to be stranger than the myth.

According to previously hidden private papers, it appears that Fawcett had no intention of ever returning to Britain and, perhaps lured by a native she-god or spirit guide whose beautiful image haunts the family archive, he planned instead to set up a commune in the jungle, based on a bizarre cult.

'The English go native very easily,' he once wrote. 'There is no disgrace in it. On the contrary, in my opinion it shows a creditable regard for the real things in life.'

More than 13 separate expeditions have so far failed to discover what happened to Fawcett in the darkest Amazonian jungle and 100 people have died in the attempt. Only eight years ago a group following his footsteps into the Mato Grosso region had to be rescued after they were held hostage by Kalapalo tribesmen and put in fear of their lives. But the veil is at last lifting. After visiting this remote jungle, then gaining permission to search through Fawcett's correspondence for the first time, the theatre and television director Misha Williams now believes the other expeditions have all been travelling in the wrong direction and looking for the wrong things. Fawcett, he claims, hoped to follow what he privately described to friends and family as 'the grand scheme'. He wanted to set up a secret community which would be based on a mixture of unusual beliefs involving both the worship of his own son, Jack, and the tenets of the then-fashionable credo of theosophy.

'I can now show that there were scores of associates who were planning to go out and join Fawcett to live in a new, freer way,' said Williams, who has become a confidant of Fawcett's descendants. He has also uncovered a drawing of a beguiling and ageless 'sith' or female 'spirit guide' who he suspects is near the heart of the mystery. Appearing only to the Fawcett family and to those who try to track the expedition's path, the erotic siren draws white men into the jungle.

Williams explains that much of the uncertainty surrounding the disappearance of the colonel can be put down to the Fawcett family's own attempts to protect their father's reputation. His surviving son, Brian, even went so far as to write a bestselling book, *Exploration Fawcett*, in a deliberate effort to put up a 'smoke screen'.

Vanessa Thorpe

FOUR

MOUNTAINS

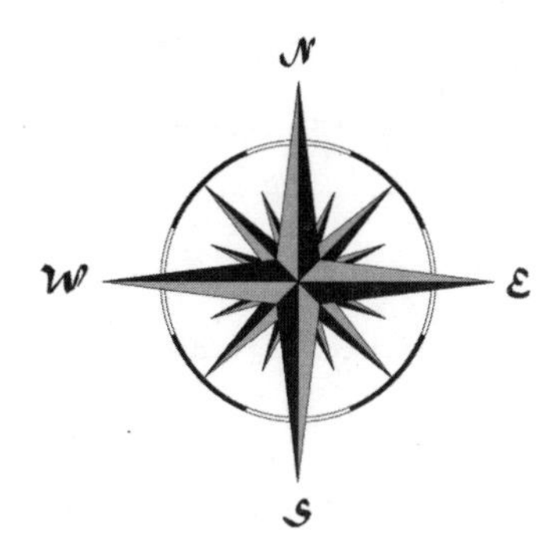

First ascent of Mont Blanc

Guardian, October 4 1837

When Jacques Balmat reached the village of Chamonix on his return, he was seized with a very severe indisposition, the effect of extreme fatigue and exposure to extreme cold. He was attended by Dr Paccard, a physician of the place, to whom, as a mark of gratitude, he communicated his discovery, offering at at the same time to show the doctor the way to the summit. The offer was accepted, and on the August 7 1786, these two daring adventurers set out from Chamonix upon this memorable expedition. They chose the route of La Côte, and reached before dark the upper part of the mountain, where they passed the night on the Glacier des Bossons. At four on the following morning they pursued their route over the ice, ascended the side of the Dome du Goute, and having reached a great height turned to the east, and passed along the ridge which is seen from Geneva, lying on the left of the summit. Here they first began to experience such intense cold, and such extreme fatigue, that Dr Paccard was almost induced to relinquish the enterprise; being, however, encouraged by Jacques Balmat, who was accustomed to such toilsome and dangerous expeditions, the doctor followed his companion.

The wind was so violent and piercing, that, in order to avoid its blowing in their faces, they were obliged to walk sideways for a considerable time. At half-past six in the evening they at length attained the summit of Mont Blanc, and stood triumphantly on a spot of ground which no one had reached before. The eyes of many in the valley had followed their track by the aid of telescopes, and the whole population on Chamonix came out to catch a glimpse of them. They remained on the summit no longer than half an hour; the cold being so intense, that their provisions were frozen in their pockets, the ink congealed in their ink-horns, and the mercury in Fahrenheit's thermometer sunk to 18 and a half degrees, or 13 and a half degrees below the freezing point. They had employed 15 hours in ascending; and though they regained the mountain of La Côte in five hours, yet they found great difficulty in descending, their sight being debilitated by the reflection from the snow. "They arrived at La Côte about midnight, after 20 hours of unremitted fatigue." Having reposed themselves two hours, they again sallied forth, and returned to Chamonix at eight in the morning. Their faces were excoriated, and their lips exceedingly swelled; Dr Paccard was almost blind, and his eyes continued to be affected for a considerable time. The King of Sardinia made Balmat a present, and a small subscription was subsequently raised for him; he was honoured also with the familiar appellation of Mont Blanc.

The fatal accident on the Matterhorn

Guardian, July 22 1865

The *Journal de Genève* of Tuesday last publishes the following letter from Randa (Valais), dated the 15th instant:

In informing you yesterday by despatch of the ascent of Mount Cervin (or Matterhorn), I did not expect it would be my duty to describe to you a terrible accident. The information which I have received respecting this catastrophe is as follows:- Messrs. Edward Whimper and Charles Hudson, members of the London Alpine Club, and Mr Haddo and Lord Francis Douglas, members of the same club, met at Zermatt, each desirous of conquering the Cervin colossus, hitherto inaccessible. Mr Hudson had brought from London cables of iron wire to facilitate the ascent, but finding Mr Whimper ready to leave he left them at the hotel, and set off with his unexpected comrades, with no other object than to find out the best way. They took with them as guides Michel Croz, of Chamonix and Zum Taugwald, of Zermatt, with his sons. It was the 13th. No member of the party expected to succeed that day; it was only proposed to find out the route which would lead to the desired object. They had, in fact, left their instruments at Zermatt, and were only supplied with seven bottles of wine. One of the sons of Taugwald left them and returned to the village.

The tourists passed the night of the 13th on the snow at the foot of the Cervin. Lord Francis Douglas, who was but 19 years of age, alone slept, overcome by fatigue; the others remained awake. At daybreak they pursued their journey, and, finding the ascent much easier than they expected, pushed on, and reached the summit towards two o'clock in the afternoon. At that time they were distinctly seen from Zermatt with the aid of a telescope. They remained on the summit until three o'clock, when they began to descend. Michel Croz went first; after him came the four tourists, Lord Douglas and Messrs. Haddo, Hudson, and Whimper, in succession. The son of Taugwald and the father closed the line.

They were all tied with the same cord, and were descending, rejoicing in their success, when Lord Douglas suddenly slipped, and, giving a violent shock to the cord, threw down in their turn Messrs. Haddo, Hudson, and all the band, who were hurried with frightful rapidity to the brink of a precipice. Taugwald sen., the last of the chain, preserved his presence of mind. He was happily able to pass his cord over the ridge of a rock, and for a moment he thought he had stopped a frightful fall; but the cord broke between Messrs. Whimper and Hudson, and the four unfortunate men, Michel Croz, Lord Francis Douglas, and Messrs. Haddo and Hudson bounded from rock to rock down a height of nearly 4,000ft. The three survivors returned to Zermatt this morning at ten o'clock, I leave you to imagine in what condition. Twenty men immediately left to discover the bodies, which they thought they could see through a glass, lying two by two, the cord having, it appeared, broke

The Matterhorn

again. The whole village and the numerous tourists there are in a state of consternation.

The bodies of the victims of the catastrophe were recovered the same day. The Rev. Mr Downdon, the English chaplain at Geneva, has left that city for Zermatt.

The *Journal de Genève* remarks: This sad catastrophe, which will excite in every part of our country the profoundest sympathy, will ever be associated with the first ascent of Mont Cervin. It was the only summit of the Monte Rosa group which had resisted the efforts of man, the last virgin summit of the environs of Zermatt, the Gablehorn, having been climbed on the 7th of this month.

Aiguille Sans Nom: making the unclimbable easy

Guardian, August 24 1898

A correspondent sends word that one of the last peaks – or rather pinnacles or buttresses, for all the true peaks were climbed long ago – to hold out against climbers in the Chamonix regions has been forced to give in. It is the Aiguille Sans Nom, and the successful mountaineer is the Duke of the Abruzzi, the late Mr Mummery's companion in the ascent of the Matterhorn by one of the untried and fantastically difficult routes which that great climber loved to work out. The Aiguille Sans Nom is absurdly named, for it is not strictly an Aiguille and it is not nameless. It is a great cliff standing out of the serrated ridge between the Aiguille du Dru and the noble Aiguille Verte. From almost any readily attainable point of view it looks less difficult than its neighbour the Pic Sans Nom, the sharp, black spike of rock to whose base Messrs. Carr, Morse and Wicks gained access in 1890, when it was first climbed, by cutting steps for some four or five hours, if we remember rightly, up the steep ice in the gully between the Pic and the Aiguille. The Duke of the Abruzzi and his guides seem to have taken to the gully, also full of ice, on the other side of the Aiguille Sans Nom, between it and the main mass of the Aiguille Verte, the way vividly described by Mr Mummery in his account of the ascent of the Aiguille Verte from this side. This part of the ascent must have been very long and laborious. In all probability it involved many hours of almost continuous step-cutting on steep ice, with much risk from falling stones, and the last part of the ascent was made over extremely difficult rocks – how difficult may be gathered from the mere fact that they had remained invincible while the Grépon, on the other side of the Mer de Glace, with its abominable vertical crack, had been converted, according to Mr Mummery, from an 'inaccessible peak' into, first, 'the hardest climb in the Alps,' and, finally, 'an easy day for a lady.' It is odd how, even before the time comes for draping a mountain with fixed ropes, blasting its awkward protuberances, and driving in iron spikes where there is not much hold without, the mere fact that it has been climbed by one party almost always leads others to climb it with comparative ease. There can be little doubt that the Aiguille Sans Nom, now that it has been once climbed, will go the way that the Matterhorn has gone and that the Aiguille du Grépon is going.

Mr Savage Landor's barbarous treatment in Tibet

Guardian, October 5 1898

Mr Landor has communicated to the press the following report in the results of an inquiry into the treatment he was subjected to by the Tibetans during his ill-fated attempt to reach Lhasa in the spring of 1897. The report was drawn up under instructions from the Government of India by Mr Larkin, the frontier magistrate:

Suddenly without any warning, the Tibetans rushed on Mr Landor and his two servants, and, overwhelming them by numbers, made prisoners of them. They cruelly bound their surprised victims. Then a number of soldiers (who had lain in ambush) arrived and took over the prisoners. The first person to be dealt with was the bearer Chanden Singh. He was accused of having taken his master into Tibet. He was questioned as to this and also as to the maps and sketches found with Mr Landor's things. Hearing the Tibetans accuse the bearer, Mr Landor called out that his servant was in no way responsible for his having entered Tibet. Thereupon a Lama struck him (Mr Landor) a blow on the head with the butt-end of his riding whip. Chanden Singh was then tied down and flogged. He received 200 lashes with whips, wielded by two Lamas. Then the prisoners were kept apart for the night, bound with cords.

Next day, Mr Landor was placed on a horse, seated on a spiked pack-saddle. Mansing [Landor's coolie] was put on a barebacked horse. Mr Landor's arms were secured behind his back. Thus they were taken off at a gallop towards Galshie. When the party were nearing that place they came up with a party of Lamas awaiting them by the roadside. Here Mr Landor's horse was whipped and urged to the front. A kneeling soldier, his musket resting in a prop, fired at Mr Landor as he went past. The shot failed to take effect ...

Arriving at Galshin Mr Landor was torn off his pony. He was in a bleeding state, the spikes in the pack-saddle having severely wounded his back. He asked for a few minutes respite, but was jeeringly told by his guards that it was superfluous as he was to be beheaded in a few minutes. He was then taken, his legs stretched as far as they could be forced apart, and then tied to the sharp edge of a log shaped like a prism. The cords were bound so tightly that they cut into the flesh. Then a person name Nerha, the secretary of the Tokchim Tarjum, seized Mr

Landor by the hair of his head, and the chief official, termed the Pombo, came up with a red-hot iron, which he placed in very close proximity to Mr Landor's eyes. The heat was so intense that for some moments Mr Landor felt as if his eyes had been scorched out. He had been placed so close that it burned his nose. The Pombo next took a matchlock, which he rested on his victim's forehead and then discharged upwards. The shock was consequently very much felt. Handing an empty gun to an attendant soldier, the Pombo took a twin-handed sword. He laid the sharp edge on the side of his victim's neck as if to measure the distance to make a true blow. Then, wielding the sword aloft, he made it whiz past Mr Landor's neck. Then he repeated in the other side of the neck.

After this tragic performance, Mr Landor was thrown to the ground and a cloth put over his head and face to prevent his seeing what was being done to his servant, Mansing. This must have been done to make Mr Landor believe that Mansing was being executed. After a short time the cloth was removed, and Mr Landor beheld his servant, with his legs stretched, tied to the same log.

Mr Landor was kept for 21 hours in this trying position, legs stretched as far as possible and arms bound to a pole, and Mansing for 12 hours. To add to their misery, they were kept in the rain, and were afterwards seated in a pool of water … When Mr Landor's legs were unloosed from their cords they were so numbed and swollen that for 15 hours he did not recover the use of them, and feared they were mortifying … On the afternoon of the third day at Galshi the two prisoners were taken on foot to Toxem. It was a very trying march, inasmuch as several rivers had to be crossed.

The prisoners were eventually released and Landor went on to write a best-selling account of his ordeal.

The Bolivian Andes

Guardian, July 23 1901

The Bolivian Andes, by Sir Martin Conway (Harper and Brothers, 12s. 6d)

There is a freshness in Sir Martin Conway's narrative which is at once surprising and delightful in so experienced a traveller. The chapters which deal with the voyage across the Caribbean Sea, the journey across the Isthmus of Panama, the rush from Lima up the wonderful Oroya line, the journey to La Paz, and the later chapters which deal with the rubber industry and the gold and tin mines should not be skipped by the reader who wants to get on to the mountaineering. The two mountains, or rather massifs, attacked were the Illimani and Sorata, the latter often called Illampu, the giants of the Cordillera Real, or inner chain of the Bolivian Andes, both sanctified by centuries of legend and worship. Illimani, the profile of which rather recalls the Jungfrau, surrendered at the first assault. Sir Martin Conway was accompanied by two excellent Swiss guides, but the Indian porters proved sadly unequal to their task. Some excuse, however, may be made for these unfortunate wretches. They were called upon to ascend a cliff 'about equal in difficulty to that of the ordinary route up any of the harder Zermatt mountains.' Supernatural terrors were added to physical, for the god was expected to avenge the violation of his sanctuary. At a final and peculiarly forbidding 'chimney' they dropped their loads, flung off their rope, and fled. Sir Martin and his guides, however, made their way to an upper camp, and the next day, after an exciting climb of 9 and a half hours, reached the summit at an altitude of 21,200 feet. On the way down, at the foot of another of the peaks of Illimani, Sir Martin had an eerie experience:

'My hand touched something soft and clammy lying on the rock beside me. What could there be of that sort in such a place? I picked it up. It was a rotten piece of Indian woollen cord swollen to the thickness of one's wrist. Tradition asserts that many years ago an Indian desperately dared to invade the secret places of the great god Illimani. He was last seen from below seated on this point where now we sat. He never came back to the abodes of men, for the god turned him into stone.'

The peak above, Sir Martin called Pico del Indio. After his triumph on Illimani Sir Martin attacked the rival, and probably higher, peak of Sorata. The first time he was turned back by bad weather; on the second occasion he was within an ace of success. The porters had broken down again, and the baggage was dragged up on sledges to nearly 20,000 feet, where the night was spent. The start was made on a moonless night over a hard-frozen and badly crevassed snow-slope, with here and there sunken snow-bridges, some 10 to 20 feet below the surface. Bad enough by day, it was an almost desperate venture by the light of a single candle, and that it was done at all speaks volumes for the trained senses of the three mountaineers.

The snow on the steep final peak proved to be in the worst possible condition, but nevertheless dawn found them within 600 feet of the summit. The prospect it revealed was seen to be hopeless. 'Huge masses of ice overhung in cliffs 100 feet high. Vast crevasses split the face across.' Little more than 300 feet from the summit a great crevasse, 50 feet wide and extending across the whole slope, made it clear that to go further with the snow in such condition was madness. An avalanche would have precipitated them into the abyss. Nothing was left but to turn back, and this was reluctantly done.

Missionaries in Tibet

Guardian, January 7 1902

With the Tibetans in Tent and Temple, by Susie Carson Rijnhart, MD (Oliphant, Anderson, and Ferrier, 6s)

A pathetic story is unfolded in Mrs Rijnhart's account of four years' missionary work in Tibet. Accompanied by her husband, a missionary of some experience in Chinese Tibet, Mrs Rijnhart first began work at Lusar, in the vicinity of the great lamserai of Kumbum, with its 4,000 lamas. The missionaries found little difficulty in establishing cordial relations with the inmates, and when a Mahometan insurrection broke out they were invited to reside in the lamaserai, where they remained for 10 months. They thus had exceptional opportunities for seeing the inner life of the lamaserai; but they failed, as Mrs Rijnhart remarks, to come on any traces of the mahatmas. It can hardly be doubted that if the Rijnharts had decided to remain at Lusar a successful mission might have been inaugurated, but both felt called to pioneer work.

A move was made to Taukar, a town on one of the great caravan routes to Lhasa. Here a son was born, and the life was varied by visits from such travellers as Captain Wellby and Dr Sven Hedin. Both husband and wife, however, were determined to push on to Lhasa, and in the spring of 1898, with an infant in arms, the start was made along the Chang-lan, or long road, which crosses the Tsaidam, to Lhasa. The hardships encountered told severely on all; the child died, and the pioneers were finally stopped at Nagchuka and ordered either to retrace their steps or to make for Ta-chien-lu, recently described by Mr Archibald Little, by the tea road. The latter alternative was chosen, but ill luck pursued the party. The transport beasts broke down, the guides were either ignorant or treacherous, and finally abandoned the Rijnharts to their fate at the hands of the robbers who infest these mountain fastnesses. Mr Rijnhart was murdered, but his wife succeeded in making her way back to relative civilisation at Ta-chien-lu. The book is above the average of missionary narratives, and the accounts of the lamaserai and tent life are interesting and vivid. The map, however, is indescribably bad.

Indian explorers in Tibet

Guardian, November 20 1903

A correspondent telegraphs from London: In writing of Tibet last night I mentioned the mass of information obtained through trained Indian explorers who entered the country in disguise and returned with their maps and reports. But the work of these men has been so extraordinary that a little more may be usefully said about them. The idea of training them and sending them into Tibet was first carried out in the early sixties by Colonel Walker, the head of the Indian Trigonometrical Survey. He selected men from his staff with some knowledge of the border languages, taught them the use of simple surveying instruments, and gave them general instructions as to the route they were to follow if possible and the nature of the information they were to obtain. Then they secretly took their departure, and for months – on one occasion for years – were lost to the world amongst the mountains and plateaus of Tibet. In time they returned, frequently having done something very different from that which they had started to do; sometimes having done little, sometimes having performed feats unparalleled before or since in travel in high Asia. Their reports were written, and such portions as could be published appeared in Indian official reports, and the travellers, so to speak, wandered through geographical literature as 'A,' 'C,' 'K,' 'No.9,' and so on, but their true names were only known to one or two men in the world, and they were not likely to tell. In later years, when the travellers retired full of years and honours, the same secrecy was not necessary, and in two instances the names became know.

The greatest of all these native explorers, perhaps the greatest traveller in Asia in the last century, was the first. He started on his extraordinary career as 'A.' He ended it by appearing before the world in his true name of Nain Singh, a gold medallist of the Royal Geographical Society and the owner of a village in the Punjab granted to him in addition to a pension by the Government of India for his services. He first reached Lhasa, disguised as a clerk to a Tibetan merchant, in 1805. He began his journey as the legal agent to some Nepalese merchants having large claims at Lhasa, and was forced back. A second time he tried by another pass, and was again driven back, but on the third occasion he succeeded, and has left an elaborate report on the route from Nepal to Lhasa, including the famous ring-shaped Lake of Palti, about 24,000 feet above the level of the sea. He saw the grand lama, a boy of 13, and after some months in the sacred city made his way back to India. Soon afterwards he and a companion journeyed to the chief Tibetan goldfields and investigated that industry.

In 1874 he was again in Lhasa, having started from Leh, in Kashmir, and he actually crossed Tibet from west to east, emerging after nine months' absence in Assam. He only stayed two days in Lhasa, as he had reason to fear that he had been discovered. On this journey he travelled 1,200 miles through regions hitherto unknown, showed the existence of a vast range of mountains to the north of the Himalayas, and did much else of a like nature, which earned for him the honours and rewards I have mentioned. Several other letters of the alphabet and numbers were wandering about Tibet at the same time, performing feats of endurance, hardihood, and skill which are known only to the students of geography and are embalmed in Indian official reports. Nerve was the first requisite of all these men, and the moment one showed want of nerve he was never seen again.

Thus by the devotion and enterprise of these men the Indian authorities have acquired a greater knowledge of Tibet than exists anywhere else in the world. Twenty or thirty years hence we may perhaps learn that in the year 1903 agents of the Indian government were scattered far and wide over Tibet, studying the geography, trade, religion, administration, intrigues around the grand lama, and much else of a similar nature. In fact, I believe that little goes on in any part of central Asia, from the Caspian to the Great Wall of China, that is not duly reported to Calcutta by some agent on the spot.

The conquest of the highest mountain in the empire

Guardian, December 7 1907

Dr Tom G Longstaff has just returned to England on the conclusion of an interesting expedition in the Himalayas. The chief feature of this journey, which lasted six months, was the ascent of Trisul (23,406ft.), this being the first occasion on which this mountain has been attempted. Dr Longstaff said: –

'The expedition consisted of Major the Hon C G Bruce (5th Gurkha Rifles), Mr A. L. Mumm (late secretary of the Alpine Club), and myself. We had with us two Italian guides, one Swiss guide, a native officer of the 5th Gurkhas, and eight riflemen of the same regiment. Originally the object of our journey was to attempt the ascent of Mount Everest, from the Tibetan side; but for political reasons we found this to be impossible, the home government having forbidden any travellers to cross the frontier. Our plans were subsequently changed, and we decided to go to the central Himalayas, to Garhwal, and from that point attempt Trisul, which I had reconnoitred in 1905.

We immediately started on our journey, marching through the foothills for a distance of 100 miles to the mouth of the Rishi Valley, the only possible route for reaching our objective, the giant mountain Trisul. We proceeded by the valley for four marches, which consisted of a series of steep ascents and descents across the various ravines. Camping at 11,600ft, on the edge of the tree line, we sent our coolies back to their villages, there being no food whatever for them in the valley. After this we had to carry our own loads and provisions.

We now began the actual ascent of the mountain. After two marches along the Trisul glacier, we started up the snow slopes of the mountain on June 7, and that evening reached a height of 20,000ft. Our tents were placed on an absolute desert of snow. Here we had to spend two nights, the wind and snow preventing any attempt on the peak. We remained huddled up in our tents. It was impossible to stay outside, and equally impossible to melt snow for drinking purposes. The wind also was so high that the stoves would not work, and, of course, we could not light them in our tents, which were only 3ft 6in high. During this period I had by far the worst experience in my foreign travels. On the third day, there being no sign of improvement, we were forced to descend to the foot of the mountain, and again camped at 11,600ft. Owing to the hardships and bad food, Mr Mumm became seriously indisposed, and, greatly to my disappointment, was unable to join me in a further attempt to reach the summit.

At 6.20 on the morning of June 11, with two Italian guides, Subadar Karbir and myself left the camp and marched rapidly along our old track, camping the same afternoon on the snowfields of Trisul, this time at a height of 17,450 feet; for I had decided that our best chance of reaching the summit was to endeavour to rush the ascent from a comparatively low camp. On the following morning we tried to leave at four o'clock, but the intense cold drove us back to our sleeping bags. We started at 5.30am, and five hours later reached our highest camp of 20,000 feet in the height of a cold westerly gale. As dangerous crevasses, half covered with snow and ice, were ahead, we roped ourselves together, and at noon reached 21,000 feet. At this time I felt the cold more severely than ever. The slopes, too, were very steep, and at times I was rendered almost breathless. My companions, however, showed no ill-effects from the altitude. Our beards and moustaches were masses of ice. We were now following the narrow NNE ridge of Trisul, which leads straight to the summit, and gradually as we approached the top all the neighbouring mountains except Nanda Devi sank beneath us.

The magnificent southern cliffs of this mountain were almost bare of snow owing to the steepness. At 4pm, after ten hours' continuous climbing, we reached the summit; but ahead was an overhanging cornice, and until I looked over this I could not be satisfied that we had actually attained the highest peak of the mountain. The cold was so bitter that we found it only possible to remain for 15 minutes …

Having planted a small flag, made out of a piece of the tent, we hurriedly commenced the descent. This began at 4.30, but I was so done up that I remember very little of what immediately followed. As darkness was fast closing in, we pushed on with all speed, and at 7.30 reached camp.

Was it victory?

Guardian, July 15 1924

The third act of the attack on Everest is over; the curtain falls on a tragedy, perhaps on a triumph. Mr Odell, in his report to Colonel Norton, throws considerable, though not a complete, light upon the last desperate push made by Mr Mallory and Mr Irvine. Through his glasses we can see the small black figures, belated but ascending, reaching as the afternoon wore on to the base of the final pyramid, known to be short and believed to be easy. And then, as Mr. Odell looked for the supreme thrust upward, there came the film of cloud which has kept the mountain's secret. That victory was attained is considered probable by the man best qualified to judge, and we can only hope that his estimate of a sleeping, painless death for the night-trapped but victorious climbers is indeed the true solution. Terrible as that supposition is, it does not rob the victims of a swift savouring of their superb achievement as they rested for a moment on the pinnacle of the world and of their high ambition …

… The amount of progress made is not be measured in feet only. When this year's expedition started there was no definite agreement about the necessity of oxygen. Now there is the most accurate information, gained by sharp experience, as to the incidence of atmospheric pressure up to the height of 28,000 feet. Should it be thought wise to attempt a consolidation of these gains and a confirmation of victory, the staff work about supplies and porterage will greatly eased.

All the climbers are suffering from heart-trouble by continued work at great heights. It is for them to decide whether the certification of triumph over Everest demands another battle.

Leader

A Woman Adventurer

Guardian, August 1 1927

My Journey to Lhasa by Alexandra David-Neel (Heinemann, 21s)

Mme David-Neel has made many adventurous travels and explorations in remote parts of Asia. She has now achieved the distinction of being the first white woman who has succeeded in reaching the forbidden capital of Tibet. In Asiatic languages and Buddhist literature and philosophy she is well know to orientalists as an accomplished scholar. In 1912 she entered Tibet from Sikkim, and a few years later reached Shigaste, the seat of the Tashi Lama. She was then expelled from Tibet, one gathers, on the representations of the British authorities. She determined to penetrate to Lhasa, not because she particularly wanted to go there, but because of the prohibition which closes Tibet to European travellers. Many had been stopped on their way to Lhasa, and had accepted failure. She would not. She was determined, she says, to show what a woman can do. And she did it!

Accompanied by a young lama of the 'red' sect, whom she had adopted as a son, she set forth from Mongolia in the guise of a Tibetan woman pilgrim, travelling on foot. Together, the intrepid pair crossed the mountains and desolate plains, often in peril from storms, robbers, and wild beasts, experiencing many hardships, living the life of the common people. Eventually they reached Lhasa after a journey lasting eight months. Still undiscovered, she continued her journey towards the frontier of British India. Arrived at Gyantse, the farthest outpost of the British sphere of influence in that direction, she went to the dak bungalow and revealed her identity. 'The first gentleman who saw me, and heard a Tibetan woman addressing him in English was dumbfounded,' she says. Thence she passed safely down to Calcutta.

As a book of travel the work is of intense interest. As a record of indomitable achievement it is unsurpassed.

J.E.E.

the history of mountaineering. Expert Alpinists hold the Eiger's north wall to be the most fearsome in the Alps. Not only has its inviolability hitherto been amply protected with the normal complement of sudden storms and avalanches which defend the High Alps, but it is for all practical purposes precipitous for the last 7,000 feet of its 13,000. So many fine mountaineers had lost their lives in attempts on it that it was believed to be virtually unscalable. After three days on the face, last week's party only got through by the skin of their teeth, the climb culminating in a blinding blizzard. It may help to illuminate the magnitude of their achievement to recall the details of the most dramatic of all the attempts to climb the north wall – the 1935 climb, which came so near to success and ended so tragically.

The party in that year consisted of two young but experienced Bavarian mountaineers, Max Sedlmayer and Karl Mehringer. The local Grindelwald or Scheidegg guides, whom no one could accuse of lack of personal courage, told them they would almost certainly be killed. They were undismayed, studied their intended route with meticulous care, and waited – fatally as it turned out – during a whole fine fortnight for 'really settled' weather.

Then at 4.30 on a late August morning they started. Like the latest party, they set off from Alpiglen at the point known to British skiers as the end of the White Hare run. Like last week's climbers, they employed a method of conquering the precipitous limestone which is frowned on by classical alpinists, but indispensable for a face like the Eiger Nordwand. The leader drove in 30 iron pitons. Then his companion climbed up these, pulling them out, climbed over the leader's back, took the lead in turn, and drove in the pegs. It is heart-breakingly slow work when every minute is precious. Still from below it seemed that they were going well in the rock. It was on the ice that they were fatally slow, cutting only one step in five minutes instead of four or five.

The second day the pace of the climb – they had covered only half the distance the first day – slowed considerably. And well it might after a night's 'rest' such as they had had. Only those who have just climbed the north face and lived to tell the tale can appreciate what they must have endured. While the sun was actually on the rock wall, water from melting snow and ice would have been pouring down their necks and down their sleeves, to become unpleasantly cold in the shadow and to freeze at night. They were climbing light and, therefore without the comfort of even a little warm food. There was no room for a proper bivouac. So they slept dangling in a rope cradle from one peg and with a knee crooked over another and a sheer drop of thousands of feet below them. And, on top of it all, the unremitting perpendicular climb.

On the fourth day of such mountaineering – when they must have been utterly exhausted but when their goal was in sight – the weather broke in sudden violent thunderstorms which became blizzards above the snow line. Anybody who, in the security of the Grindelwald valley, has heard the terrifying roar of the wind across the north face of the Eiger in a storm, can imagine what it meant for the climbers dangling on the rock face. The Germans retreated from their highest point to a snow ledge under an overhanging rock. There when the storm spent itself, Col. Udel, the famous air ace, and Fritz Steuri, the Grindelwald guide, saw one of the climbers from a plane. The other climber, Fritz, told me, was apparently in his sleeping-bag under the snow, and had probably died first. The climber who was visible appeared to be sitting on his ruck-sack beside his companion. Snow came almost up to his waist. There he had been frozen – his face turned towards the Scheidegg, as if looking for the help which he must have known could never have reached him. And there, until the heavy snows of winter hid him from the morbidly curious with their telescopes, he could still be seen.

Since then the north wall has warded off half a dozen other attempts, and claimed at least twice that number of victims. Now it has been conquered. It was as inevitable that it should be, as it is inevitable that one day Everest will be conquered. It is in the nature of man to attempt the unattempted at whatever cost to himself, and the mountaineer feels (however unconsciously) with the poet: –

That merely by climbing, the shadow is made less
That we have some engagement with a star
Only to be hounoured with death's bitterness
And where the inaccessible godheads are.

Of Human Endurance

Observer, November 9 1952

Annapurna by Maurice Herzog (Cape, 15s)

This is the story of the French Himalayan Expedition, told by its leader, who, with one companion, achieved the summit of Annapurna (26,493 feet), the highest point on this planet ever reached by a human being. It was an astonishing feat, and M. Herzog's account of it is very graphic and, in the later stages, very moving.

It was an astonishing feat for many reasons. The French, a well-found and experienced party, entered Nepal with two alternative objectives. Both were peaks of over 8,000 metres and both (it was hoped) were within striking distance of the same base. Reconnaissance of Dhaulagiri showed it to be impregnable. There remained Annapurna. But where was Annapurna, and how did one get there? The Survey of India map was demonstrably misleading. Which of the many towering ridges that they scanned from below masked their objective? M Herzog, like a huntsman casting for a scent he has lost, deployed the expedition widely; at length, on May 23 1950, they confronted the north face of Annapurna, and could descry what looked like a possible route to the summit. The monsoon was due to break exactly a fortnight later.

The French, loyally seconded by their Sherpas under Angtharkay, attacked the mountain with great dash and consummate skill. Five intermediate camps were established, the last of them at over 25,000 feet, and on June 3 Herzog and Lachenal, in a supreme effort, reached the summit. At those heights men's minds work slowly and inconsequently; and as they began the descent Herzog, stopping to open his rucksack for some purpose which he could not remember, dropped his gloves. They rolled down the slope and disappeared. He had a spare pair of socks with him, but in his light-headed, slow-witted state it did not occur to him to protect his hands with those. He even forgot that he had lost his gloves. It was only when he reached the first camp that he read in the eyes of his comrades the lesson that he had to learn: 'My fingers were violet and white, and as hard as wood.' Lachenal's feet, also, were frost-bitten.

The weather was breaking, the visibility was nil. The four men descending painfully from camp V, missed camp IV and spent a night of agony in a crevasse. Swollen feet could no longer be coaxed back into frozen boots. Dark glasses were lost, and two of the party were snow-blind. The monsoon, mercifully a few days late, was beginning. The doctor's skill, the Frenchmen's courage, and the staunchness of the Sherpas saved – just saved – the retreat from being a disaster; but it was an ordeal of the utmost rigour, and M. Herzog, his body racked and his spirit all but broken by arterial injections of novocaine and other drugs, his wounds suppurating through his bandages as he was carried for day after day over appalling country, suffered worse than any of them.

His account of all this is unaffected, and is stamped by nobility and truth. The early part of his narrative, describing the complex and often simultaneous operations of a number of reconnaissance parties, is not particularly rewarding, and the difficulty of following it is increased by the author's practice, which seems to be de rigueur for French travel-writers, of relying extensively on reconstructed conversations. But the conquest of Annapurna and the bitter sequel to it make an enthralling story, and the story is admirably told. There are some good illustrations, and my only quarrel with the translators is over their failure to realise that sac, in mountaineering contexts, should seldom be translated 'sack.'

Peter Fleming

Everest notebook: Down from the heights

Observer, June 21 1953

That molehill Everest has begotten such a mountain of controversy as almost to awaken this once forbidden city from its long sleep. The conquest of the great lonely snow peak by a small band of dedicated men is an achievement forgotten in the chatter of political dispute over returning heroes.

Everest should have been situated anywhere else but in Asia – or perhaps anywhere else in Asia but in Nepal. From a vast mass of people whose two certain common feelings are frustration at the lack of material achievement and a consequent natural jealousy of Europeans who have so long dominated them there has arisen one man: Sherpa Tensing Norgay, who has gained a clear-cut physical triumph that the whole world perforce recognises as unique.

The effect, at any rate in India and Nepal, has been electric. Unheeded go Hillary's brilliant Alpine work that led Tensing to the summit, Hunt's masterly planning and his firm reiteration that he regards his team as one unbreakable unit in the victory. If and when Tensing himself publicly states that he was not first to set foot on the ultimate peak, an overwhelming mass of public opinion will not believe him. Already, responsible Indians here are talking of Tensing's silence being bought by the British. In a valley where landlords possess their own private gods to whom tenants pay dutiful tribute it is easy enough to build a world of make-believe.

Though the government of West Bengal, the Indian province in which Tensing lives, has been careful enough to issue a press statement claiming the Sherpa as an Indian citizen, to Nepalis, downtrodden for so long under feudal rule, he epitomises a resurgent Nepal. 'Has he taken out Indian naturalisation papers?' one of them asked me fiercely. 'Even if he says he's Indian when he arrives here he was Nepali when he climbed Everest.'

But Nepalis, whose battles in history have usually been among themselves, are, as they ruefully admit, poorly organised to celebrate an international triumph. Their approach is best exemplified by the half-uniformed policemen who stand at the corners of the rutted roads around the city and who, when you car rattles towards them, do not wave you on but portentously hold up imaginary traffic coming from the other direction. Thus, while an Indian newspaper with proud black headlines is raising a fund to build Tensing a house at Darjeeling, not even Mrs Tensing knew when I spoke to her that a Nepali fund to build her and her husband a house in Katmandu has already, despite the country's poverty, reached a sum three times as great.

The Indian embassy is maintaining a calm and masterly correctness amid this diplomatic tension. When Mrs Tensing, a broad, twinkling, self-possessed woman who sensibly wants to know where the money is coming from, asked for accommodation, the Indian embassy tactfully referred her to the Nepal government, who wished to make her a state guest. And thus she is comfortably installed in the state guest house with an ADC to attend her – which must have surprised Tensing when he reached here, for before the expedition he was housed in the servants' quarters of the British embassy, which resemble nothing as much as a row of stables with a farmyard outside. Indeed, the British (for the Swiss treated Tensing as the social equal of other members of their expedition) are coming out somewhat poorly here from what might once have been supposed to be their own exclusive triumph.

It is not presumably the fault of Ambassador Summerhayes that Tensing was not offered a knighthood – an omission which has violently offended nationalist Nepalis – but he has become inextricably involved in a battle of the British press which has hugely delighted Asian onlookers, and, incidentally, has been responsible for many of the misinterpretations which Colonel Hunt so rightly deprecates.

No reasonable person grudges the *Times*, with its long record of support for Everest expeditions, its copyright on the story. But when Mr Summerhayes began to take upon himself the decision as to how many newspaper correspondents should be allowed into Nepal he became intimately involved in the struggle. The first of the *Times* correspondents was innocently granted a visa by the Nepal government on the ambassador's recommendation that he was a member of the mountaineering party. The *Daily Telegraph* was conducted in through official channels, though those channels have since been stiffly dammed. Reuters apparently received official sanction and proceeded to establish a radio monitoring service of telegraphy between Nepal and India that revealed to them every press message sent out from Kathmandu.

The total result has been a monumental mass of guesswork which almost obscured the simple, magnificent fact that a devoted band of mountaineers had struggled to the highest point in the world. The gaunt, austere figure of the ambassador attempting sometimes by rather unorthodox methods to keep the story as his own personal exclusive has gloriously added to the confusion. King Tribhuvan of Nepal and his new prime minister, who have been puzzling over which of four classes of the Nepal Star to offer Hunt and Hillary, in view of Britain's apparent intention to 'fob off' Tensing with the George medal, must indeed be grateful that this is an epic which can never be repeated.

Rawle Knox, in Katmandu

A bucaneer in the North-West Frontier

Observer, October 26 1958

A Short Walk in the Hindu Kush by Eric Newby (Secker and Warburg, 25s)

If Mr Eric Newby had been born a hundred years ago he would almost inevitably have gravitated towards the North-West Frontier of India. Finding the life of a fashion salesman uncongenial, in 1956 he sent, on the spur of the moment, a laconic telegram to an enterprising friend in the foreign service with some knowledge of Asia. 'Can you,' it read, 'travel Nuristan June?' Nuristan, which is the tract of country north-east of Kabul, is not altogether unknown, but it is hard, arid country and few modern travellers have thought it worth while to travel there. The main objective of this two-man party was a 20,000-ft peak which, strangely, they very nearly climbed. Strangely, because Mr Newby's previous mountaineering experience was confined to a weekend's practice in Wales with two maids from the local inn.

A Short Walk in the Hindu Kush will horrify conventional mountain explorers and even less ambitious travellers with some sense of organisation. Nevertheless, this is quite the funniest travel book I have ever read. Mr Newby has a wonderful acute ear for dialogue, and the continuous contrast between his buccaneering self and his somewhat priggish companion is consistently amusing. It is impossible to read this book without laughing out aloud.

John Morris

Top of the world

Observer, September 6 1959

Joe Brown is a plumber from Manchester. He is 28, a short, unobtrusive, sociable man with a rather large triangular face capped with thick black hair. He is 5ft 6in in height, weighs approximately 9½st, and the only thing outwardly unusual about him are the scars on the back of his hands. Brown, over the past six years, has become the most highly regarded mountaineer of the decade. This has been a vintage summer for British mountaineering and to the men who have been climbing the most terrifyingly difficult routes in Europe, Brown is, by inspiration and example, the unquestioned leader.

He is certainly the best rock climber in Britain – in a higher class than either Sir John Hunt or Sir Edmund Hillary – and as a mountaineer he is among the best six in the world. Their fame rests on their organising ability, their skill in judging conditions on a big mountain, their capacity to keep moving for long periods under difficult conditions. Brown shares these qualities with them; but on a rock face he is also, as they are not, a human fly. He has made climbs go which, until he did them, were thought impossible. Besides, Brown is a supreme example of the way, since the war, young members of the working class have broken through into sports hitherto the preserve of the professional classes. 'Everest wasn't for the likes of me. Only university men or army officers or people with money were invited.' In the 30s Brown's only playground would have been the outcrops of gritty rock that jut up like the spines of a perch along the Pennines – outcrops within easy reach of the great industrial centres of the North. But in the 50s his horizon has been extended from Wales to the Alps and, in 1955, the Himalayas, where he climbed Kanchenjunga, the third highest mountain in the world.

Joseph Brown was born in Manchester on September 26, 1930, the youngest of a family of seven children. His father was in the building trade but died when Joe was eight months old. His mother brought the family up alone. Joe was too young to know much of the struggle.

He started camping and 'messing around in the countryside' when he was 12, but it wasn't until the bleak and snowbound winter of 1946-47 that he first went into the hills. His first rock climb was on Kinder Scout, the highest top in the Pennines. He had no equipment except a pair of gym shoes and a 1in. brewer's rope. The second time out he borrowed his mother's clothes-line.

Later that year Joe Brown and three school friends went on their first expedition. They took one tin of food per person per meal, sewed up some tarpaulins into sleeping-bags and set out for a fortnight. The four 16-year-olds, carrying 112lb. on their backs (a weight even a Sherpa porter would baulk at), took three days to cross from Eskdale over Scafell into Wasdale and over the Black Sail Pass to Pillar Rock. Most of the time they drew a straight line on the map and carried their loads wherever this course took them. They lasted for nine days before their food ran out. They climbed nearly everything in sight with Brown always leading. He even did one short 'very severe' climb – the top classification at the time.

He was called up in 1949 and served in the RAOC – a year in England and a year in Singapore. Although he has fallen nine times when climbing, a distance of 300ft. on one occasion, he had his only serious accident in the army. The tea urn was brought into the hut, there was a rush, and Brown broke his leg in three places. He says that he has never really been afraid on a mountain. 'When you are in control of everything, climbing is as safe as any other activity, but then perhaps the weather turns really bad. You get number and you know the position is serious but you are not really afraid. Perhaps it's because I've never been anywhere where I thought that I couldn't get down.'

During his leaves and after his demobilisation Brown climbed all the hardest routes in Britain. But the horizon was getting too small. He set about widening it. Clogwyn du Arddu, the hardest cliff in Wales, had thirteen routes on it (all were classified as 'severe' or 'very severe'), and it was considered that every possible weakness in the rock had been explored. Brown began to probe where no one had been before, perfecting a technique of hand jamming – placing his hand in a thin vertical crack and then closing the thumb across the palm so that the hand became jammed.

'You can hang from the fingers of one hand for about three minutes, but I can last double that time with a good hand jam. People thought that it was a navvy's trick for those with rough hands, but they soon found that done properly it doesn't hurt at all except when you have got to turn your hand in the crack.' Soon the cliff had fifty routes on it and two more classifications, 'exceptionally severe' and 'excessively severe' had been added to the climbers' vocabulary. 'A proper jam,' he says, 'is magnificent. It makes you feel rested and relaxed.'

In 1954 Brown made the second ascent of the west face of the Dru – the vertical, smooth, 4,000ft spire in the Mont Blanc range that had taken the first party of Italians seven days to climb. In adverse conditions, Joe

Brown and his friend Don Whillans (another plumber), did it in two days. No British climber had done anything considered so hard for 20 years or more, in relation to the ruling standard.

Eight months later, in 1955, Joe Brown, plumber extraordinary from Manchester, and George Band, ex-president of the Cambridge University mountaineering club, made the final and successful assault on the 28,000ft summit of Kanchenjunga, then the highest unclimbed mountain in the world. The working-class school of climbing and the university class had worked together successfully for the first time.

A year later Brown was in the Himalayas again on the Muztagh Tower – a spire as fearsome as the Dru but more than 10,000 feet higher. 'Certainly it was hard stuff. It took us three or four days to climb one section of 1,000 feet. You could drop a stone over the edge of the ridge and it wouldn't hit anything for 4,000 feet.' Exposure doesn't affect him much. 'On bad rock it can bother you but on good rock it doesn't worry you at all. The airy position is something you enjoy. It makes a climb. You think 'Whee, we are up here in the air.''

Just before he left for Kanchengjunga, Joe set up in business in Manchester on his own as a property repairer and plumber. He had been earning about £7 a week and thought he could do better by himself. It was hard for the first six months but then work began to come in regularly. In 1957 he married a school-teacher and they started to buy a modern, three-bedroomed semi-detached house not far from his mother's home.

Already Joe Brown is a legend amongst British mountaineers. He knows this but it has left him unaffected. His friends are the same people who climbed with him in the early days, a Runyon-like bunch known by their nicknames – Dirty Black Jack, Ox, The Villain, Mortimore, Count Neddie, Able, Fred the Ted, Matey, Beardie. Every Wednesday evening they gather at Joe's house, play cards, talk about last weekend, the weekend to come.

He pokes gentle fun at the old social order. When Sir Edmund Hillary asked him what he would do if he climbed Kanchenjunga he replied slowly, 'I'll ask you, Ed, to call me Sir Joseph.' One of his most constant climbing companions is a smaller edition of himself, an electrical engineer called Joe Smith, who hitch hiked to France at the age of 15, climbed Mont Blanc and hitch hiked back. Two Joes became somewhat confusing so Joe Brown named him Mortimore 'because it sounded like one of those names these university types are always calling each other.'

And why does he climb? 'They asked Mallory that question and he said, 'Because the mountains are there.' I reckon he was just stalling them off. No other sport brings people so close together. If you climb with a man for a week or two you know everything about him. Then there's the pure physical pleasure when you are on form. The movement and the balance so that you are really sorry when the climb comes to an end. When you have done a good climb, you feel really pleased in yourself and the way that you are climbing.

'Perhaps if I had done more ski-ing or fishing or underwater swimming I might like them as much but then there is not the companionship. And the beauty, too. Even at 28,000ft on Kanchenjunga, with your breath squeezing out and your throat feeling as if the skin had been taken off it, you'd have to be a mug not to appreciate the surroundings – the world below you and Everest 90 miles away as clear as anything. Nothing adds up to all this.'

Human Resources

Observer, May 5 1974

Alive: The story of the Andes Survivors by Piers Paul Read (Alison Press/ Secker and Warburg, £3)

On October 13 1972 an aeroplane carrying a Uruguayan rugby team and their friends left Montevideo for Santiago de Chile. Even the very beginning is mildly odd, for although Uruguay is a famous soccer country, rugby is a recent and exotic import from Ireland. Nearly all the young men were ex-pupils of the Stella Maris College; nearly all were the children of rich, conservative, devoutly Catholic parents; all felt themselves somewhat apart (and superior) because of their devotion to a game which had never taken on in their own country. It wouldn't be unfair to write that although these young men were physically tough, and in excellent condition, many of them were also spoilt darlings who had been accustomed to living off the fat of an increasingly lean country.

Over the Andes the aircraft got lost in a dense patch of cloud, hit a series of air-pockets and crashed. Many of the passengers were killed at once; others were badly injured. But by a remarkable fluke the fuselage of the aeroplane, although deprived of its tail and one wing on the very first impact, slid to a final stop in a remote, snow-covered valley; and more than half the passengers were virtually uninjured. The survivors did what they could to help the injured, to make their freezing 'quarters' habitable and to ration the very meagre supply of available food. But the badly injured died one by one, usually in agony; the food ran out; they heard on a transistor radio that the search for them had been called off after 10 days.

There was still a major disaster in store for them. After a few weeks an avalanche fell on the fuselage and buried a large number of those who were still alive and well – more or less. Several of the buried died before their companions could dig them out; and eventually only 16 were left, all male; all except one, under 30. It was resolved that the strongest members of the party, physically and mentally, should be given specially good treatment – fed better than the others, rested, mentally fortified – and that these three would set off for the west in search of help as soon as the weather began to improve.

In the event only two made the attempt. After an almost incredible 10-day journey over a high and still snow-covered mountain this tiny expeditionary force came down into a Chilean valley, found a small farm and were able to explain where their companions could be found. The other 14 survivors were then rescued by helicopter, on the seventy-second day after the plane had crashed.

Something fishy here? Yes, in a sense, as journalists and others were fairly quick to suspect when the 16 survivors arrived in Santiago. Not that most of the young men were particularly reluctant to explain what so obviously needed explaining. At a fairly early stage in their appalling ordeal it had been decided that they would eat the dead bodies which surrounded them, and which had been – fairly well – preserved by the intense cold.

At first I wasn't sure that Piers Paul Read had been wise to concentrate so much on the cannibalistic element in this story. But he soon persuaded me that the nauseating details were not there just to titilate our ugh-faculties. The cannibalism is a wonderfully successful symbol of the underlying theme of the whole book; the extraordinary will to survive exhibited by most of these young men; their courage, tenacity and ingenuity even at the most terrible and bitterly discouraging moments. What is remarkable is how quickly most of them became completely accustomed to their unfamiliar diet – there are periodic rows, for example, because one or two of the survivors have a tendency to hog more than their fair share of the rations.

These young men had two great advantages over the average man or woman in the same situation; they were extremely fit and they were mostly religious believers of varying degrees of intensity and conviction. Their passionate faith that God was watching over them tells us nothing about whether He was or not; but it reminds us again that one of the many uses of belief is that it can provide comfort and strength when these are most needed.

But Mr Read's most notable achievement has been to bring to vivid life at least 30 individual human beings, and to show us, in great detail, how some 12 of them reacted to the dreadful circumstances in which they were suddenly placed. One criticism which is less trivial, I believe, than it might seem at first sight. Mr Read reveals by his vocabulary that he knows and cares nothing about rugby football. But it would have been interesting and enlightening to be told the position of each player involved, and also something about his style of play. Sometimes *le jeu, c'est l'homme*; though not, perhaps, quite as often as most sports enthusiasts believe.

Philip Toynbee

The Ice Chimney – *Lyric Studio, Hammersmith*

Guardian, November 19 1980

The Ice Chimney centres on the life and death of Maurice Wilson, who set out in the mid 1930s to climb Mount Everest, alone and without training or oxygen, and perished in the attempt. Barry Collins' retelling of the story is rather more than staged biography, however; he has tried to raise the haunted, obsessive and ultimately quixotic figure of Wilson into a paradigm of spiritual struggle; to subsume history into the less timebound realism of poetry.

Certainly Wilson was a strange and fascinating character. The son of a Bradford mill-manager, he revolted instinctively against the trammels of class; a war hero who refused to settle into the stifling compromises of civilian life; a messianic figure tormented by a feverish sexual imagination. After curing himself of TB by fasting almost to death, he became convinced that he had a mission to set an example to mankind. Later he challenged Gandhi to a fast.

He met implacable opposition to his Everest plan from the establishment. He taught himself to fly, and entered Tibet in disguise. When his body was found at the foot of the North Col in 1935, he appeared to have died within walking distance of a food dump and shouting distance of his sherpas. Also found were two diaries – one detailing his attempt to climb the mountain, another relating his somewhat tormented sexual fantasies – and various items of women's clothing. Given these facts, it might have been tempting to resort to some psychoanalytical proposition. Collins decisively rejects the reduction of his protagonist's behaviour to mere pathology, although a pathological pattern is strongly suggested. But his account is more complex and more ambiguous.

Visually, the play is almost entirely static: status is central. Everything depends on language, upon the articulation of Wilson's tumultuous inner life. It is a major risk to load any play in this way, and here it almost pays off.

Hugo Davenport

Messner beats the mountain giants

Observer, October 26 1986

A man who has climbed Everest, alone and without recourse to that artificial stimulant, bottled oxygen, could be deemed to have done it all. Yet the world's foremost mountaineer, Reinhold Messner, actually had something a shade more outrageous up his insulated sleeve. A confessed self publicist, the Austro-Italian who owns a castle near Bolzano in the South Tyrol has in fact made two oxygen-free ascents of the highest peak. First by the South Col trade route in 1978 with Austrian friend Peter Habeler, then solo two years later from the Chinese north.

Remarkable achievements, but they slip modestly into perspective with the news from Katmandu last week of his latest conquest, Llotse (27,890 feet), an Everest neighbour. Messner, aged 42, is now the only climber to add all of the earth's 14 mountains of 8,000 metres to his personal collection. Llotse is the last silver medallion on a shining string coveted by every international aspirant in what is often mistakenly assumed to be a non-competitive activity.

Only 20 years or so ago, the idea that a climber would boast ascents not merely of every Himalayan giant over 26,000 feet but some of them solo and all on standard leg and lung power would have been thought wildly romantic. Or more likely not-quite-science-fiction. Apart from the inordinate luck, competence, fitness and drive needed to accomplish such a quest, it was feared by medical experts in altitude physiology that serious brain cell damage would afflict anyone climbing long at such rarified heights without support of oxygen.

The risk is there, but Reinhold strode a step ahead of conventional thinking almost since he began climbing with his schoolmaster father and brothers in the Dolomites at the age of five. His usual pragmatic approach told him that bottled oxygen brought the summit down to climbers, not climbers up to summits. To test his tolerance in thin air he once sat with his oxygen mask on his knee during a high altitude flight, ignoring the pilot's alarm. The tall, dark and often dogmatic climber graduated in architecture at Padua but the qualifications that distinguish him today are Everest, K2, Kangchenjunga, Makalu, Nanga Parbat, Annapurna, et al.

They were won on a long, hard and at times harrowing apprenticeship that cost him some toes from frostbite and his younger brother Gunther in an avalanche on the epic traverse of Nanga Parbat in 1970. His marriage to the elegant Uschi also collapsed under the strain of his hectic writing, lecturing and media itinerary and incessant expeditions. A clutch of attractive, mountain-orientated women followed, the latest being Nena Holguin, a warm Canadian who accompanied him with their baby on a recent sell-out British lecture tour.

Messner brought athleticism to climbing the major peaks of the world, running daily 3,000 feet uphill in under 40 minutes from his home high in the Tyrol, an Austrian district absorbed into Italy after the first world war. He climbed some of the most formidable Dolomite rock routes alone and later wrote an essay while still in his 20s that helped redirect the whole course of climbing. *The Murder of the Impossible* chastised those who sought to eliminate risk, carrying their courage in their rucksacks. By this he meant artificial climbing gear that virtually ensured success on any Alpine mountain face.

Reinhold has carried that ethic to the Himalaya, the arena he turned to when the loss of his toes largely excluded him from the technical rock and ice climbs of the Alps, which he extols in his book *The Seventh Grade*. The surprising thing is that Messner has recently refused to acknowledge that completion of the 14 peaks above 8,000 metres was his life's goal, an achievement that today amazes and will remain the envy of so many. Denying any intent to be a super-Munro bagger, a mere collector of summits, Messner tells his critics that his aim was not simply to slog up great mountains, tucking eight-thousanders under his belt. 'I am more proud of the manner in which I did them,' he said.

Nanga Parbat (26,658 feet), the German icon in the Karakoram, climbed in 1978 alone without oxygen by a new route, is almost certainly the jewel in his mountain crown. Hidden Peak (26,470 feet) in stylish Alpine mode with Peter Habeler, or the Eigerwand in a record 10 hours with the same partner, these are his own special terms of reference.

Flying home last week to his Italian castle the much sponsored mountaineer may reflect that as his prestige soars the heavy demands on his life are bound to intensify. And though he need never take a major risk in future for a crust, his mountain quests are sure to go on. Neither tragedy or triumph have diverted him in the past.

Alan Thomson

Obituary: Göran Kropp

Guardian, October 5 2002

'I wanted an adventure that was truly unprecedented,' said Göran Kropp, who has died in a climbing accident aged 35, and in 1996 he achieved just that. Climbing on to his bicycle in his native Sweden, his gear packed in panniers and a trailer, he pedalled off to Nepal. There, he climbed Everest without bottled oxygen, relying only on his own strength to carry his tent and supplies up the mountain.

At base camp, extravagantly equipped American expeditions, recalled in Jon Krakauer's bestseller *Into Thin Air*, dubbed Kropp the 'crazy Swede', an image that he relished. Tall, broad and beefier than a Charolais, when Kropp gripped an ice axe, you feared for the beaches of Lincolnshire. But while most writers saw the Viking in him, the mask concealed a gentle, reflective and intelligent man, with an essential attention to detail.

Kropp's passion for mountains started early. Through binoculars, he would watch his father, a human rights lawyer, climbing on the steep limestone cliffs of the Italian Dolomites. At the age of six, he was led by his dad up Galdhoppigen, the highest peak in Norway. But after his parents divorced, his mother returned to Sweden and climbing lost its appeal. Instead, Kropp spent his teenage years in extravagant rebellion, combining a musical passion for reggae, prog rock and punk. By 16, he had his own apartment, which he painted in Rasta colours, and spent his high school years going to gigs, forming an unlikely friendship with the Swedish singer Eva Dahlgren after he cadged a lift home from her after one of her concerts. Once his appetite for partying burned out, he joined the Swedish paratroopers, where his reputation for eccentric behaviour and outrageous trials of strength was established.

Kropp met Mats Dahlin, a young soldier passionate about climbing, and, bored by military discipline, felt his old enthusiasm returning. The travel, hardship, joy and lack of regulation that mountaineering encapsulated was the natural environment for Kropp's rebellious streak. The difficulty was cash. Earning a pittance in the army, he abandoned his apartment and moved into a tent pitched in a gravel pit close to the barracks. He dreamt up surreal tests of endurance to train for the mountains. Setting his alarm clock randomly, he would rise at 3am and march 30km in full kit; if it was 6am, he would march 60km.

Kropp's career began in isolation, his ambitions gleaned from books, and his talent was geared more towards the grand gesture than technical brilliance. He and Dahlin drew up a list of progressively higher mountains as a plan to reach 8,000 metres, the so-called 'death zone'. Along the way, Kropp became absorbed in the unconventional and risky lifestyle. He contracted typhoid in Ecuador, and lay delirious and alone in a dosshouse. In the next bed was a man with a pistol under his pillow who claimed to be Bruce Lee's brother. In Kathmandu, Kropp married a Nepali woman to qualify for a cheaper Everest permit. He took up paragliding and, when the money started to flow, bought a share in a racing car.

In 1993, after becoming the first Swede to climb K2, he left the army and hit the lecture circuit with extrovert, self-mocking performances. He loved being on stage, and debunking the inflated egos of mediocre climbers swarming over Everest. Kropp's ebullience, however, got him into trouble. He lost a libel action in London after confusing the names of two British climbers in his autobiography, accusing the wrong man of liking a drink. Then, after he shot a polar bear while trekking to the North Pole, the Swedish press turned against him, and he moved to Seattle.

Behind the stage performances and booming laughter, Kropp was a sensitive soul, deeply affected by the death of his climbing partner Dahlin while training in the Alps. He was also a highly intelligent organiser with an appetite for the latest technology. But while some of his competitors used these advances to repeat old challenges more easily, Kropp wanted to push limits. His Everest climb was the supreme example of this trait. It mixed meticulous attention to detail with the serendipity his personality seemed to generate. On the trip out, he found lodgings in a Hungarian brothel, and was routinely stoned as he pedalled through Iran. On the mountain itself, he returned for a summit run three times before success came, an astonishing effort for a man breathing only the thin air of altitude. At base camp, his fiancee Renata Chlumska, an Everest climber herself, waited anxiously as Kropp came close to death struggling to the summit. The irony of his death, falling from a routine, 70ft rock climb near his home in Seattle, is too much.

Göran Kropp, mountaineer and adventurer; born November 12 1966, died September 30 2002.

Ed Douglas

How a climber cut off his arm to save himself

Guardian, May 9 2003

The climber who cut off his own arm to free himself from a boulder, yesterday told the excruciating story of his ordeal, describing how he planned and undertook the hour-long amputation using a cheap pocket-knife after five days stranded in the mountains of Utah. Aron Ralston, 27, from Aspen, Colorado, was exploring a canyon in the Canyonlands National Park on Monday last week when the boulder fell on him, trapping both of his arms. After freeing his left one, he said yesterday, he tried every method he could think of, including chipping away at the rock with the knife, before concluding that his only option was 'actually severing my arm' below the elbow.

On the Tuesday, finishing the last of the water he was carrying, he made his first attempt, preparing a tourniquet from a pair of bike shorts. 'Essentially I got my surgical table ready and applied the knife to my arm, and started sawing back and forth,' he told reporters at the hospital in Grand Junction, Utah, where he has been recovering. 'I didn't even break the skin. I couldn't even cut the hair off of my arm, the knife was so dull.'

Later, he 'got so far as to puncture the skin, and then found that I couldn't cut the bone, essentially knowing that you can't cut the bone without a bone saw,' Mr Ralston said. 'By Thursday I'd figured out an option around that ... I was able to first snap the radius and then within another few minutes snap the ulna at the wrist and from there, I had the knife out and applied the tourniquet and went to task. It was a process that took about an hour.'

He applied the tourniquet, made it to the base of the canyon, drank water from a stream and began to hike out of the park. He was discovered by two Dutch tourists who gave him food and water and helped him to a helicopter that had been searching for him.

'I'm not sure how I handled it,' said Mr Ralston. The stump of his right arm, which he wore in a sling, has already been fitted for a prosthetic attachment. 'I felt pain and I coped with it. I moved on.'

In a press conference full of barely imaginable detail, the person least agonised by the retelling seemed to be Mr Ralston himself, who related it in a matter-of-fact tone, interspersed with lighthearted asides, that began to hint at the degree of detached calm and mental strength the operation would have required. The knife, he noted at one point, was 'essentially the kind of thing you'd get if you bought a $15 flashlight and you got a free multi-use tool'. And on landing in the helicopter in the town of Moab, he said, he 'walked off the helicopter to a gurney, and started filing my report with the national park service folks who were waiting'.

He added that he was 'looking forward to getting back to those wonderful mountains and canyons of the Rocky Mountain West'.

Oliver Burkeman

FIVE

OCEANS

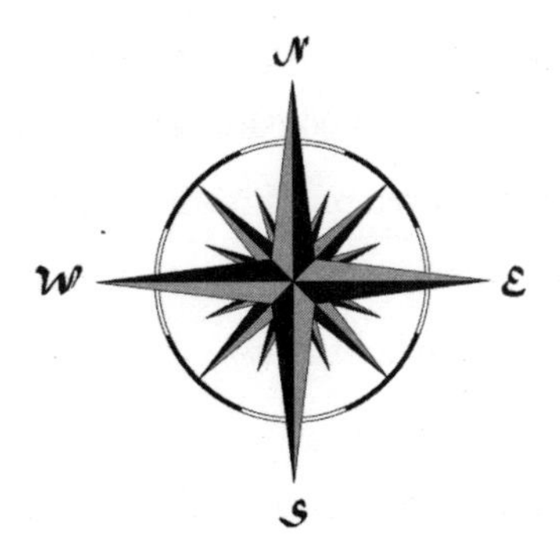

Captain Webb swims the Channel

Guardian, August 26 1875

Captain Webb's second attempt to swim across the Channel has been successful. He started from the Admiralty Pier in Dover at four and a half minutes to one yesterday afternoon, when the wind and tide were in his favour. He was not in such a perfect state of training as when he made his first experiment. He was accompanied by two rowing boats and a lugger carrying the representatives of the press. The lugger was under the command of Mr Toms, who acted as pilot.

Under the instructions of Toms, Webb dived into the sea whilst the tide was at its ebb, and he was carried by it in a westwardly direction. He commenced with and maintained during the journey the chest stroke, and made an average of from 18 to 20 strokes a minute, his movements indicating from first to last that he was not only a man of great strength, but that he was also a graceful swimmer. By 1.30 Captain Webb had made excellent progress. Mr Payne and Mr Wilkinson, the referees, estimated his speed at the rate of a mile and a half an hour. He indulged in refreshments, in the shape of half a pint of beer, at a quarter to three, receiving the stimulant from his cousin, who was in one of the rowing boats. He was then about three miles from the Admiralty Pier, and was passed by the afternoon mail packet from Calais and by the twin steamer *Castalia.* Bearings were now taken, but a slight haze prevented any satisfactory result being arrived at.

At a quarter to four o'clock Captain Webb again took some ale, and it was then agreed that he was quite five miles from Dover. The heat of the sun now became somewhat oppressive, but the fog was rapidly rising, and the Dover cliffs, which had been for some time obscured, were again visible. Captain Webb still swam vigorously, displaying better form every hour, and replied cheerfully to the inquiries made by those in the lugger every time it came within hail of him. He was occasionally surrounded by porpoises, none of which, however, came too near to him, and they all escaped the pistol shots aimed at them from the boats.

At five o'clock the captain enjoyed some beef tea, and he then proceeded to resume his task with the remark that he felt capital. He was now about six miles from Dover, and was being fast carried by the tide to the eastward, or in the direction of the Goodwin Sands. Forty minutes later he once more indulged in beef tea. He said that he did not experience any discomfort from the water, the porpoise oil with which he had anointed himself before starting no doubt proving to be a valuable means of maintaining his normal temperature. He acknowledged by a wave of his hand the cheers he received from the passengers on board a large steamer that passed him … By a quarter to eight Cap Gris Nez light was sited … At 5am he said he was all right. The French coast was then sighted for the first time. At half-past five the sun rose, and Webb took some brandy … At half past nine a service galley, rowed by men of the London, Chatham, and Dover Railway picket service, rowed from Calais harbour … The lad Baker, well known for his diving feats in London, entered the water and got alongside Webb, who was swimming gallantly, but very slowly. At 19 minutes to 11 the Captain landed on the sands, about 200 yards west of the bathing machines, at Calais, amid enthusiastic cheering from the crowd which had collected and those in the boats.

Captain Webb appeared somewhat exhausted, and stumbled as he left the water. He was immediately rubbed down and placed in a conveyance, and taken to the Hotel de Paris. Some local physicians came to him, but he said he felt warm enough, and should be all right after a sleep. They recommended him to take some port wine, and he did so, and then went to bed, where he enjoyed a sound sleep.

Dr William Beebe and His Bathysphere

Guardian, July 30 1934

No portion of the globe inhabited by living creatures is less known than the depths of the sea. Much of our knowledge of deep-sea life is based on

row of portholes along their sides. They are pink, yellow, or lavender in colour. Some of them burn with a steady radiance, while others wink or flash intermittently like theatre signs. On one dive Dr Beebe kept his searchlight going long enough to observe two zones of abundance and a wide interval of scanty, mote-like life.

Stanley Rayfield

The sea's mercy

Observer, April 2 1950

The Kon-Tiki Expedition by Thor Heyerdahl (Allen and Unwin, 12s. 6d.)

Thor Heyerdahl was a young anthropologist no one would listen to. He believed that a race responsible for the colossi of Easter Island and for the culture of Polynesia had come from Peru. He believed that the sun god Tiki, traditional ancestor of all Polynesians, was the same person as Kon-Tiki, the priest-king of a white race defeated and expelled by the Incas. According to Peruvian legend, Kon-Tiki set sail west into the Pacific with the remnant of his people and was never heard of again.

No one would listen, because such a voyage seemed incredible. Four thousand ocean miles on rafts of balsa logs? For neither Incas nor their predecessors had hollow boats. Yet, somehow, coconut-palms had got there. Geologists denied there had ever been a land-bridge.

Thor Heyerdahl decided to be his own guinea-pig. On the coast of Peru he would build a raft of balsa-wood, according to ancient patterns, and would see what happened. What happened is now incontestable fact. The Humboldt and South Equatorial currents, coupled with the south-east trades, drove the raft north and west an average of some two knots; and a hundred days after leaving Callao, Heyerdahl and his five companions grounded on a Polynesian reef!

The sea's mercy is no less spectacular than its fury. No ship is so huge or so well-found as to enjoy absolute safety at sea; true, but no craft is so small or so queer that its chances of survival are nil.

All the same, I can think of only two voyages at all comparable with that of the raft Kon-Tiki. Fred Rebell sailed from Australia 9,000 miles to California alone in an eighteen-foot Sydney harbour boat, with only a canvas hood for shelter. Rebell, like Heyerdahl, was a landsman – his only study of sailing had been in Sydney Public Library. Even more recently a Chinese sailor, whose ship was torpedoed somewhere off the Cape of Good Hope, found himself alone on a small raft practically without water or provisions. Yet five months later he drifted ashore on the coast of South America in good health. For five months he had lived 'off the country,' on raw fish and rain water.

Except for that Chinaman, has any mariner lived in such close communion with the sea and its inhabitants as these Norwegian voyagers, drifting naturally with wind and current an inch or two above the surface? It was not only that they caught, in this utterly deserted tract of ocean, varieties of fish never before seen alive – but one such fish was actually caught in a sleeping bag! For fish of all kinds were constantly jumping on board, almost into the frying pan. The voyagers grew quite matey with the sharks – feeding them on titbits or wrestling with them for sport, hauling a shark on board by the tail with their bare hands. Again, they had only to move the cabin matting and they could look straight down between the logs the raft was built of into the depths. Down at mysterious, phosphorescent creatures, bigger than elephants – how Coleridge would have rejoiced in this vivid, astounding sea-bestiary! This is a meeting with a fifty-foot whale-shark, the largest fish of all:

'Knut was staring straight into the biggest and ugliest face any of us had ever seen. The head was broad and flat like a frog's, with two small eyes right at the sides and a toad-like jaw which was four or five feet wide and had long fringes hanging drooping from the corners of the mouth ... It grinned like a bull-dog and lashed gently with its tail.'

This book is an enthralling account of an experience without parallel. At times the writing, though occasionally a little over-conscious, is very good indeed. I have no doubt at all the book will prove an immediate popular success, and no doubt either that it will outlive most successors to take its place among the classic small craft and queer-craft voyages of the world. When the time comes for that, however, I hope the author will add a few good charts, and working drawings of the raft itself (especially the arrangement of the five centre-boards), even at the expense of some of the many photographs of bare limbs and beards. So little is known, technically, about rafts. Clearly their hydraulics differ entirely from the hydraulics of a hollow hull. Every possible detail would be of scientific value. Whereas about bare limbs and beards we know plenty.

Richard Hughes

Survival

Observer, October 25 1953

The Bombard Story by Dr Alain Bombard (Deutsch, 12s 6d.)

The cruel sea in peace-time murders about 200,000 people a year. Roughly a quarter of these, according to Dr Bombard, become castaways and would have a chance of rescue if they did not succumb so quickly through hunger, thirst, exposure. He undertook a single-handed crossing of the Atlantic from east to west in a 19ft inflatable dingy in order to prove that they need not die. He named his craft, aptly, L'Hérétique.

His theory was based on the fact that the sea is much richer in food than the land. Fish caught with lines and plankton strained through a silk net would therefore provide him with a balanced diet. Fish juices and condensation would supply sufficient fresh water; and in any case, contrary to a common superstition, salt water at the rate of a pint and a half a day is tolerated by the human body for about five days before it causes nephritis. So Dr Bombard reasoned that with food and drink and the will to live a man might keep alive on a tiny raft for many weeks.

He personally demonstrated this by remaining alive for 65 days, during which he half-sailed, half-drifted from the Canaries to the West Indies. Dr Bombard's body stood up to a diet of raw fish and plankton, which tasted like lobster puree; and, most remarkable of all, Dr Bombard's mind stood up to such loneliness and terror as even the Kon-Tiki voyagers never knew.

His diary, which he prints verbatim, is a terrible document, displaying that overstrained mind at the point of disintegration. He dreams of chicken cooked with rice – for the mind at such times always fixes itself upon one particular dish. Real and imagined terrors, of storm and doldrums, of failing health, of swordfish and sea monsters, are the companions of his nights and days.

Dr Bombard survived, though by a very narrow margin, and proved something which he could never have proved in the laboratory. For there he could have tried out his theory only upon his body; he could never have tested almost to its breaking point: the unconquerable mind.

John Moore

Dive to deepest point on Earth

Observer, January 24 1960

Two men in the United States bathyscaphe *Trieste* today reached the very deepest part of the sea, diving 37,800 ft. in the Marianas trench in the Pacific. This plunge of over seven miles has taken man to a depth far greater than the height of Everest and 2,800ft. deeper than the trench was thought to be. Lieutenant Don Walsh, 28-year-old submarine officer, and his companion, Jacques Piccard, the Swiss scientist, both appeared to be in excellent condition after spending some 10 hours in a compartment 5ft 8in by 3ft 2in

They started down at 9.22pm on January 22, and reached the bottom at 2.10am on January 23. They stayed 30 minutes on the bottom, and surfaced at 5.57am on January 23 – so they took 4 hr. 48 min. to descend and 3 hr. 17min. to get back. Their teeth were chattering with cold, and they were wet through with the bathyscaphe condensation. They said they found the bottom was very soft and that they stirred up silt and what they called 'dust' when they landed. Then, in the light shining from the sphere, they saw weird white fish with popping eyes.

I talked by telephone to Lieutenant Walsh after the dive. He said:

'The assignment was to go all the way to the bottom. But you don't know that you will get there until you have reached it. Anything can go wrong. The difficulty is to come up. We could have developed a leak in the wiring system or a part of the hull could have developed a leak. We could have started losing our gasolene and losing our buoyancy very rapidly; except, of course, that the bathyscaphe is pretty solidly engineered. We did not have any trouble at all.

'It had been a very rough day on the surface. Once we got under it was a relief. Our stomachs were queezy when we started from the waves, and the bathyscape stank of gasolene. But it was nice to be quiet. The sphere itself is made of steel varying from four and a half to six inches in thickness. The interior diameter without the equipment is about six feet; but the actual working space is less. You pretty well take up your positions and stay there for the whole dive. We had equipment to measure currents, temperature, the salinity of the water, and we had depth indicators. We also had a tape recorder to take down what we saw, and we had still and movie cameras mounted in a rail before our window.

'You may pass through clouds of luminescent organisms; yesterday we saw very little of those. Off San Diego we saw streams, so that it's like floating through a shower of stars or shining snowflakes. We kept our lights on quite a bit on the way down but we saw nothing until we hit the bottom. Then a fish about a foot long, shaped like a sole, with protuberant eyes, one on each side, swam close to us. It had been thought that 25,000 feet was the deepest at which vertebrate animals could live, and here we have seen a species of a flat fish.

'We floated down like a free balloon. Our sphere was not attached to a cable. Once you dive you are on your own. You communicate with the surface by a wireless telephone that uses waves generated in the water like submarine detection equipment, like modulated sonar. There is no feeling of motion.'

After they surfaced Lieut. Don Walsh dropped a weighted plastic container with an American flag; this, it is hoped, will go straight to the deepest spot which the bathyscaphe reached.

A practical reason for investigating the deep sea trenches is that they might provide dumping spots for radioactive wastes which will accumulate in hair-raising quantities in years to come. But if there are ocean currents or living organisms in the trenches, it will be too risky to use them as radioactive dustbins.

Philip Deane

Plymouth – New York

Guardian, July 6 1962

Francis Chichester's passage from Plymouth to New York alone in his 13-ton cutter *Gipsy Moth III* in the record time of thirty-three and a half days can fairly be acclaimed as one of the great achievements of the sea. As a feat of human endurance (and at the age of 61) it is outstanding:

different in degree, for such things are incomparable, but making the same kind of sustained demand on willpower as climbing a mountain without oxygen. The gear of a 13-ton yacht, normally sailed by a crew of six, would tax the strength of most men to handle alone. Chichester has not only sailed his yacht single-handed across the Atlantic but driven himself day and night to race her. And his race was, perhaps, the purest form of human competition in that he was racing solely against himself and his own record for the same cross set up in 1960. He has failed in one sense – his personal ambition was to achieve the crossing in 30 days. But by any other standard his achievement will seem complete; and some measure of it may be gained by considering that his closest rival in the 1960 race, Colonel HG Hasler, took 48 and a half days to make the passage.

Readers of the *Guardian* have been able to follow Chichester's voyage day by day by radiotelephone. The radiotelephone is not new, but its use in a small sailing boat to speak across ocean distances is unique. At the outset of *Gipsy Moth*'s voyage it was held that if messages were received from her half way across the Atlantic it would be as much as could be reasonable hoped. About 40deg. west of Greenwich was regarded as the probable limit of radiotelephony from a small battery-operated set. New York is 73deg. 50min. west of Greenwich, and Chichester was still talking to the *Guardian* off Long Island.

This is an immense achievement for British radio engineering, and the credit goes fairly to Marconi Marine, the designers of *Gipsy*'s radio equipment, to the Exide batteries which powered it, and the marine services of the Post Office, which maintained a constant watch for *Gipsy*'s calls and made communication with her, often in conditions of great difficulty. *Gipsy*'s telephone was used to report a yachtsman's voyage, interesting and unusual, but in world terms scarcely of deep significance to humanity. The experience gained, however, is capable of being put to many uses, and the new range of radiotelephony that she has opened may serve to make life happier and safer for people in ways still unguessed. It has been a brave adventure by a brave man.

Leader

Rowing the Atlantic

Guardian, November 28 1966

The Atlantic was first crossed in a rowing boat in 1896 by two Norwegians, George Harbo and Frank Samuelson, in a Grand Banks dory. They had a savagely exhausting passage, but achieved the remarkable time of 62 days from New York to Le Havre. Their record was left unchallenged for 70 years.

It was challenged this year by two British crews, David Johnstone and John Hoare in *Puffin*, and Captain John Ridgway and Sergeant Chay Blyth, of the Parachute Regiment, in a 20-foot dory, *English Rose III.* Puffin was found drifting in mid-ocean with no sign of her crew, and it must be feared that Johnstone and Hoare have been lost. Ridgway and Blyth landed at Kilronan in the Aran Islands, on September 3, after a passage from Orleans, Cape Cod, of just under 92 days. After rowing past the outer islands of Aran, they made the last few miles to Kilronan under tow from the Aran lifeboat. Before accepting the tow both wondered if it was quite fair, if they ought not to row ashore under their own oars. A gale was blowing at the time, they were in some danger from the rockbound coast and they decided that as they had passed the outer islands of the group a tow was fair enough. Few would dispute it.

A narrative based on the logs that the two men kept on their passage is published today in *A Fighting Chance* (Paul Hamlyn, 21s). It is a supremely interesting document, not only as a factual account of a physical ordeal but for the psychological insight it offers into what prompts men to undertake such an ordeal. Both men, with their army training, were physically extremely fit. But their logs make it clear that their survival was essentially a mental and moral achievement.

Ridgway was the leader of the expedition, and he acknowledges that he got the idea from David Johnstone: when he heard of Johnstone's plans, he wanted to race him across the Atlantic. Blyth had once been Ridgway's sergeant in a parachute unit but he did not go with him because of this NCO-officer relationship. The two men had canoed together, understood each other, and trusted each other. In fact, Ridgway tried to dissuade Blyth from asking to come, because Blyth was married. But Ridgway was also married and both men's wives understood their husbands' need for adventure. (Most of the handful of men who have so far explored space are married. Perhaps marriage helps to promote the sense of responsibility imperative to the success of such adventuring.) Neither Ridgway nor Blyth was particularly good at games, but both shared a kind of moral determination to keep themselves fit, and to finish whatever they undertook. The Army certainly helped. But the Army was only part of their lives. Ridgway drew inspiration from these lines of Shelley which he wrote in his diary:

To suffer woes which hope thinks infinite,

To forgive wrongs, darker than death or night…

To defy power which seems omnipotent

Never to change, nor falter, nor repent,

This is to be good, great and joyous, beautiful and free,

This alone, life, joy, empire and victory.

When Ridgway said he wanted to row across the Atlantic and that Sergeant Blyth was willing to row with him, the army helped by giving them leave, and the RAF by finding them a couple of seats on a flight to Canada, but they were not deluged with 'official support.' Ridgway chose his boat, a Yorkshire dory, built by Bradford Boat Services, mainly because she could be bought for £185, and he did not want to extend the mortgage on his house more than he had to. They made their own way from Canada to Cape Cod by bus. The boat was an excellent choice, the keeless dory design enabling her to ride the sea rather than attempt to fight it. She was altered for the voyage by having her gunwale raised nine inches, and by having turtle decks fitted fore and aft over watertight compartments containing expanded polystyrene for additional buoyancy. Fresh water was carried in two-gallon containers under a false floor. There was no cabin, but a canvas shelter could be erected over a metal U-frame.

In this craft Ridgway and Blyth lived and rowed and slept for 92 days. Early in their voyage they met Hurricane Alma, a disaster in the sense that one third of their rations was ruined but a blessing in a way, in that having survived a hurricane they had enormous confidence in their boat. It was not until near the end of their voyage that the were

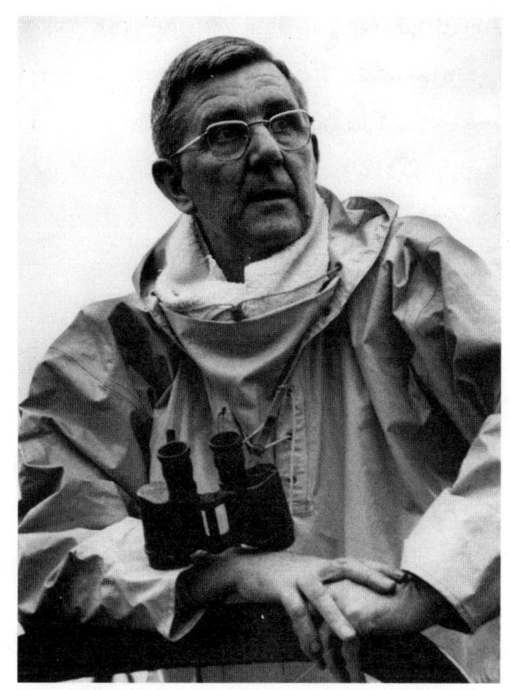

JRL Anderson

able to signal a ship (the *Haustellum*) and obtain replacements for their ruined stores – several ships passed within a few miles of them, but although they signaled and sent up flares they were often ignored (a sad comment on the standards of watchkeeping too often accepted at sea nowadays.) Until they got food from the *Haustellum* they had to live on short rations, and suffered from lack of food. Boils and sores were slow to heal, and lack of food produced a dangerous mental torpor which could be overcome only by a fierce, conscious effort.

Both men found deep comfort in prayer, and believed in divine help; several moving passages in their journals refer to this. Both also are honest. Seargeant Blyth writes: 'How strong was that faith? Well, for three weeks after we landed I didn't set foot in a church. Neither did John. Our rocklike belief began to crumble the moment our feet were back on solid ground. We feel much closer to God now than we did before setting out on our journey, but it is a pale shadow of the religious fervour that gripped us in mid-Atlantic.'

The voyage of *English Rose III* is undoubtedly of value in adding to recorded experience of prolonged physical strain and Ridgway's and Blyth's experience of survival rations will enable the services to make improvements here and there to survival kits and perhaps to survival drill. But it would be wrong to approach their adventure by asking what use it was. They set out to row across the Atlantic because they wanted to. An ambition to be called a little mad, perhaps. But it is a form of madness to make one proud of human beings.

JRL Anderson

North About

Guardian, June 9 1967

Vinland Voyage by JRL Anderson (Eyre and Spottiswoode, 45s).

In 1966, the *Guardian*'s yachting editor, Mr JRL Anderson, with a handful of more or less enthusiastic companions set sail in the 44-foot cutter *Griffin* to duplicate as far as possible what may have been a Norseman's journey that ended in the discovery of America. He was encouraged and supported financially in the venture by the *Guardian* – surely an imaginative gesture. For the journey could prove nothing except that America can be reached in a small sailing vessel, a fact that has been known for some time. The truth seems to me to be that as in the case of Heyerdahl's raft voyage across the Pacific this was an operation for which the designated object was no more than an excuse. Men have always been prone to throw themselves on to a piece of wood shaped in this way or that and try to find out what the world looks like on the other side of the horizon. There is no accounting for this impulse and no arguing against it. We feel it to be good; and we do not know why.

Griffin sailed by the way of the Faroes, Iceland, and Greenland, down to New England, which may or may not have been the place the sagas refer to as Vinland. This is a journey not commonly undertaken by a yacht; and since Mr Anderson is a professional journalist he has a sharp eye for the things the yachtsman seldom sees –

'The icefield is not quiet; there are loud explosions as the floes grind together. It is dangerous but very beautiful. The floes are in fantastic shapes – aeroplanes, ships, flowers , birds, monsters. The colours are wine-dark, purple, blue, and bottle-green. Absolutely lovely – but harrowing.'

And again –

'For all its danger to us, it was a beautiful world … surgically clean in its purity. The keystone to a line of pack would be a huge iceberg, bigger than a long street of houses, with a massiveness to dwarf an atomic power station…one floe would hit the iceberg, crashing to a stop against it; then another floe would cannon into that and so on and on, like some appalling concertina-crash on a motorway, but a crash extending for miles and with vehicles as big as hotels.'

Indeed, this was a dangerous journey, in storm and ice and fog. Mr Anderson makes vivid those things familiar to every yachtsman – the shambles of a boat sleeping too many people, the demonic spite of an auxiliary engine which will only function when it is not wanted, the mournfulness of seasickness and exhaustion, the moments of huge laughter, of magic or terror. Indeed, he made a personal discovery in the art of dead-reckoning, which should find its place with the flight of birds, the appearance of seaweed, and all the trivia by which the primitive navigator made a guess at his position. He shaved in sea water; and when the soap lathered more easily he knew the water was fresher and that the boat was in the vicinity of melting ice.

I am unable to assess the worth of the argument put forward for New England as Vinland. It turns, among other things, on the exact meaning of a number of Old Norse words; and I do not know Old Norse. I have to go by the word of the expert. I am in the position of a juror who has heard no more than the counsel for the defence and has no idea what the prosecution will say, nor how the judge will sum up. But the defence makes a good, readable book for those who go down to the sea in small boats; and whether anything has been proved or not, a fine, dangerous time was had by all.

William Golding

Sailor's heroic welcome

Guardian, April 23 1969

Robin Knox-Johnston, the first solo yachtsman to sail non-stop round the world, was resting last night after a hero's welcome from the people of

Falmouth. He completed his 30,000-mile voyage in 312 days and a Cornish harbourmaster summed up the feelings of all seafaring men as he watched the battered 32ft ketch *Suhaili*, complete the final, agonisingly slow tacks to the finishing line: 'He's a real professional,' he said. Television viewers heard Sir Francis Chichester, sailing only feet from *Suhaili*, say of Knox-Johnston : 'You can't help admiring him. The more you see of him the more you admire him. He's really playing it very cool.'

He had been escorted by a Royal Navy minesweeper and the boats of Truro and Falmouth harbourmasters, but as he neared the line, he was met by everything in Falmouth that could float – not the least of his skill was in avoiding running down the small boats. His brothers were put on board at the finishing line and drank brandy with him. He came ashore at a yacht club in a change of clothes to a salute of shots and walked unsteadily up the red carpet to meet Sir Francis Chichester. He was also welcomed by the Mayor of Falmouth, who read congratulatory telegrams from the Queen, Prince Philip, Mr Wilson and Mr Heath. Later, Sir Francis Chichester officially declared him the winner of the *Sunday Times* Golden Globe race. Knox-Johnston said he had kept going when he did not think he had a chance of winning, but the news in Australia that he was in the lead had encouraged him.

Max. Poss. Error

Observer, July 12 1970

The Strange Voyage of Donald Crowhurst by Nicholas Tomalin and Ron Hall (Hodder and Stoughton, 38s)

Once I saw scrawled on a can of film the words 'dawn for dusk.' It gave me a great feeling of ecstasy. I felt like Archimedes after his famous discovery in the bath, and wanted to jump and shout for joy. Here, I thought, is the message of the media in its simplest and most mystical terms. The extraordinary story that Messrs Nicholas Tomalin and Ron Hall have to tell expounds the same theme. They tell it brilliantly, with commendable consideration and compassion for all concerned; especially for Crowhurst and his wife, Clare. For me, their narrative goes with the one telling how Claud Eatherley was made crazed with contrition for the atomic bomb he didn't drop on Hiroshima; essential documents of our time.

Though the public memory nowadays is notoriously short, probably most people will remember the round-the-world non-stop sailing contest organised some two years ago by the *Sunday Times*, and how one of the contestants – Donald Crowhurst – after, as it appeared, putting up a very gallant show, disappeared without trace on what purported to be the last lap of his voyage. His boat, a trimaran, *Teignmouth Electron*, was found drifting in mid-Atlantic with no one aboard. Three logbooks in the cabin, on examination, showed that Crowhurst's round-the-world voyage was a complete hoax, sustained by phoney radio messages he had transmitted from time to time. There was also in the cabin some film and sound recordings he had made for the BBC. What was clear beyond any shadow of doubt was that Crowhurst had sent himself in imagination round Cape Horn and on to the Antipodes, while he lurked in the Atlantic to meet up there with this imaginary self; with the idea that then, having kept the rendezvous, he would return triumphantly to Teignmouth, the winner of the race and a national hero.

Tomalin and Hall show how carefully and ingeniously Crowhurst worked out his imaginary voyage, and the subtlety with which he reported on it to his assiduous press agent in Teignmouth, Rodney Hallworth. A lot of this care and ingenuity was really wasted. When he slipped up – as he occasionally did – no one seems to have noticed, with the exception of Sir Francis Chichester who was dubious from the beginning, and, of course, knew the form. It is interesting to speculate on whether, if Crowhurst had carried the hoax through to the end, he would have been found out. Personally, I rather doubt it. Witness the enduring reputation of TE Lawrence, the strong chorus of credulity that greeted *Papillon.* Deceptions, like beauty, are in the eye of the beholder; in the kingdom of fantasy, only the fantasist is believable.

Crowhurst, however, was no ordinary fantasist. Otherwise, with his gifts, he would not have wasted his time trying to sail round the world. The field of politics, of television, of advertising, of socio-academics was wide open to him. There was something off-beat about him; something unusual, amounting at times to a kind of genius, which held him back from these lucrative and greatly admired pursuits. In his last logbook writings Crowhurst deals at length – some 25,000 words – with certain mystical-philosophical notions which have assailed him, to the point that he believes he has experienced a great and unique revelation, sent to him from God via Einstein, and qualifying him to claim divine status himself.

It all reads, I agree, pretty crazily, and is taken by Tomalin and Hall as signifying Crowhurst's final mental collapse. In this, we are told, they are supported by psychiatrists to whom they have submitted the text. I am myself not so sure. If, say, Blake's *Prophetic Books* had been likewise submitted to psychiatrists, would they not have concluded that he was raving? It is possible that Crowhurst, far from becoming mad, became sane, and that it was his sanity which led him to disengage from the fantasy his life had become in the only possible way – by taking a header into the Sargasso Sea through which he was then, most appropriately, sailing, and letting *Teignmouth Electron* go on alone. There is, admittedly, no final proof that this is what happened, though, as Tomalin and Hall point out, some veiled references in the logbook may well be taken as pointing to such an intention. It is difficult, anyway, to think of any other possible ending.

I hope very much that some time the full text of Crowhurst's Prophetic Book will be made available. The extracts given, and the perceptive commentary provided, create an impression of an energetic but rather commonplace mind carried out of its own restricted dimensions, and, as it were, threshing about in an unfamiliar stratosphere. There are some images and phrases which somehow rise out of their own banality, like a sunset over Croydon. For instance, the game of cosmic chess, which is so difficult to follow because 'God is playing with one set of rules, and the Devil with the other exactly opposite set of rules.' Or, evil as the 'choice of interpretation of symbols.' Or this:

'There is such beauty in truth that I am prepared to submit to the discipline I hated most, the rigid, unmoving, stupid, bigoted system called the Holy Roman Catholic Church, because the pure mathematics fit any place any time.'

Mad? Certainly perplexing, and in some way troubling. Thinking of Crowhurst in his last extremity, I found myself saying, as Dorothy Parker did when she saw the stricken cadaver of Scott Fitzgerald: 'The poor son of a bitch!' At one point in his musings, Crowhurst found that his clock had stopped, so that he didn't know what time it was – or, for that matter, what day of the week it was, or where he was. Turning back to his tables to work out the time, he reached the conclusion that is must be 4.10am Greenwich Mean Time. Then, looking outside, he saw that it was broad daylight, with the sun high in the sky, and wrote in his logbook: MAX POSS ERROR. So, dawn for dusk, or dusk for dawn. No matter.

Crowhurst was born in India, of Anglo-Indian parentage, and went to school there. His father, like so many Anglo-Indians, worked on the railways; his mother seems to have been fanatically, if not hysterically, religious, and belonged to the Jehovah's Witnesses. It was something of a Kim-like upbringing. When the Raj came to an end the bottom fell out of their world and the family decamped with the sahibs and settled in England, where their circumstances were poor. One detects a touch of Alf Garnett in the father, who succumbed fairly early on to a heart attack. The mother became ever more shrill and complaining, and finally had to be put into an old people's home. A tough background, calculated to produce duplicity, and alternating moods of over-confidence and self-deprecation.

It will be remembered that Kim in Kipling's story serves a guru as well as his sahib masters. It is the yogi side that comes out in Crowhurst's last meandering thoughts, with more of the *Upanishads* than of Einstein in them. If a film is made – and what a theme! – I should hope that the final plunge into the Sargasso Sea would not be just because his electronic toys had broken, and the BBC was awaiting him at Teignmouth. There ought to be some flavour, as well, of the funeral pyre, and banks of flowers, and mantras chanted, and time dissolving into little wraiths of fragrant smoke.

Malcolm Muggeridge

Ripping but not jolly

Guardian, July 17 1980

High Mountains and Cold Seas: A biography of HW Tilman by JRL Anderson (Gollancz, £9.95).

HW Tilman's advice to young men wanting to get on to an expedition was simply: put on your boots and go. He went. He fought on the Somme and at Ypres and earned an MC and bar ('Isn't it great about the jolly old MC?') and then took himself off to become a settler in Kenya ('It's a ripping country') where, having broken new ground, he looked about for something more to do. At the age of 31, he met Eric Shipton and climbed Kilimanjaro with him. It was the start of a legendary partnership. (Years later, in the Karakoram or somewhere, Shipton remarked 'Is it not time you called me Eric?' Tilman replied: 'No.' 'Why?' said Shipton. 'Because it's such a damn silly name.')

Tilman was probably the first man to cross Africa on a bicycle. He injured his back in a Lakeland fall in 1932 and crawled on all fours for help for his companions, and his doctors told him he would never climb again. He crept off to the Alps and remained ramrod straight. He remained straight-backed and as tough as old boots to the end. He climbed Nanda Devi in 1936 and led the '38 Everest expedition. In the next war he saw Dunkirk, Alamein and Tunis and then wangled himself into being dropped behind enemy lines to fight with the partisans in Albania. Later, he did the same in Italy, earning the DSO. After the war he journeyed and climbed in Central Asia and Nepal, and became an improbable consul in Burma.

At 56, he bought an old pilot cutter: in 14 years he sailed 114,000 miles in her. He crossed the Patagonian ice cap and circumnavigated South America, he sailed round Africa, and off the Arctic regions and South Georgia. He lost her off Jan Mayen Island. He bought another, and lost her four years later off Greenland. He bought another, and went north again. At 79, three years ago, he set off for the South Shetlands for another expedition. There has been no word since.

He never sought publicity or sponsorship, and he never made a fuss. He didn't like people who made a fuss. 'It is a question whether those who contribute nothing towards the expenses of a voyage, have any right to complain,' he wrote once, of a crew member who protested about being offered leftover curry for breakfast in the Antarctic! He wrote 15 books, but his biographer concedes that he gave nothing much away: mountaineers apparently admire the climbing books and yachtsmen the sailing ones, but for us, the stay-at-home types, the excitement is pruned away in a dry, deprecating narrative.

It's a key to why this man's marvellous life hasn't actually resulted in a marvellous biography: Tilman just didn't want to be marvelled at. Never mind about the 'jolly old MC' from the Western Front: the young veteran of the Somme was just keeping his guard up. He kept his guard up all the way from Ypres to his septuagenarian daredevilry off Spitzbengen. He never married; he was normally taciturn even with his friends. JRL Anderson's biography is a careful, honest study which remains curiously unrevealing, nonetheless, being written in a slightly cramped, circumspect style, as if the author were afraid that one day his old friend might pop up, and accuse him of making a fuss…

Tim Radford

Weather eye makes Ellen simply the best
Guardian, February 12 2001

Quite simply, Ellen MacArthur is the best oceangoing sailor Britain has ever produced. She may have been beaten to the line by Michel Desjoyeaux, but that should not detract from the scale of her achievement. The Vendée Globe is the toughest race in the sailing world. To finish it in a little over 94 days, 12 days faster than the previous record, is testament to a huge talent. At the age of 24, a decade after she came to the sport, this was a milestone performance. For the past three months, MacArthur has been on her own, skippering a 60ft yacht, that would ordinarily be crewed by 11 people, in the foulest conditions. She has survived the freezing south Atlantic and the blistering hot tropics. To achieve this calls for remarkable mental and physical strength. To do so at the speed MacArthur has demands an even more astonishing level of skill, courage and belief.

It is the ability to read the weather that marks out the exceptional sailor, and MacArthur is blessed with a particular skill. Her superior interpretation of the same meteorological information that every sailor in the race had was one of the keys to her success. Once they have digested all the data that appears on their computer screens, great sailors will study the clouds and make their decisions about what the wind will do. Her knack at predicting accurately where the wind will be strongest and in the right direction, is uncanny. It is this skill that enabled her to track down Desjoyeaux as they sailed up the east coast of South America. About 1,000 miles off Rio de Janeiro, she detected that a high pressure system had moved further west than normal and was heading for where she thought the strongest winds would be. She was right, and made up

600 miles in three or four days. Her other great skill is as an engineer. This includes dealing with the boat's sophisticated electronics as well as repairing sails and rigging.

The race winner, Desjoyeaux, appeared baffled by what MacArthur had achieved. 'Ellen is a great mystery to me,' he said. 'She is 10 years younger than me and she could have beaten me.'

'She's achieved the unachievable,' said Sir Peter Blake, who has won the Whitbread round-the-world race and the America's Cup. 'For someone of her age to do this gives a huge direction to other young people.'

With the world at her feet, MacArthur will announce her forthcoming plans today. They are likely to include the French 60ft trimaran offshore circuit. We may not know a huge amount about that particular series in Britain, but if MacArthur has her way – and she usually does – we soon will.

Bob Fisher

When man takes on nature

Observer, June 10 2007

It is not so much a sport, more a state of mind. A myth that happens to be real. A mix of miracle, madness and self-murder. Surfing is many things to many people, but even this highly symbolic ritual, rooted in a Polynesian tradition dating back more than a thousand years, is not immune to the forces of globalisation. Big-wave surfing in particular (minimum 20ft waves) was long the monopolistic reserve of Hawaii, and notably of Waimea Bay on the North Shore of Oahu, which once had a claim to being not just the premier big-wave spot in the world but the one-and-only.

But as the Billabong XXL Big Wave Awards (the Oscars of hardcore surfing) at Anaheim, California, in April attested, there are now serious rivals not just on the West Coast, but on coasts north, south, and east too, in Australia, South Africa, Spain, Mexico, Chile and Tahiti. So much so that the whole show has been rebranded as the Global Big Wave Awards.

The past decade or two have seen a revolution not just in terms of diffusion, but also of inflation. As recently as the late 1980s, any claims much beyond 30ft were fanciful. Now the standard is 60ft-plus, perhaps 70 (last year's winner weighed in at 68). It is true that the system of measurement has shifted from the approximate and elusive 'vertical' from base to crest to the more accessible but oxymoronic 'face-height', thus automatically upping the ante. But it is also true that the waves now in surfers' sights are genuinely bigger than the waves of yore. Thanks to the advent of the jetski, the surfer can be 'towed in' to joust with behemoths the like of which would be otherwise unmakeable.

Without wanting to sound like King Canute in the face of an unstoppable tide, I would like to recall an era when there was no awards ceremony, it was understood that mere numbers are not the whole story and everybody already knew who was numero uno anyway. In the 1970s it was Eddie Aikau, native Hawaiian, and lifeguard at Waimea. When he died heroically at sea in 1978, Ken Bradshaw moved in and muscled his way to pre-eminence. A Texan linebacker in origin, he bullied 20ft-plus monsters into submission. He would bite chunks out of the boards of surfers who got in his way. He had long hair and a bushy beard and looked as if he could part the waters not just ride them.

Then, in the winter of 1982-83, Mark Foo dropped in. The new kid on the block was younger, lighter, Chinese-American, more of a Bruce

Lee in shorts. He didn't set out to do battle with 30ft waves, he danced with them, he finessed them. Foo and Bradshaw were bound to clash. Waimea was not big enough for both of them. One day, Bradshaw, convinced that Foo had 'stolen' one of 'his' waves, dunked him and tore his board to bits with his bare hands, and possibly his teeth. Thus began the duel between Bradshaw and Foo, the old guard and the young gun, that would last more than a decade.

Foo heaped scorn on 'the men with beards'. And he had a smooth, good-looking, fast-talking media presence: his own surfing column, a radio show, television broadcasts, appearances in feature films. He was the first on the North Shore to acquire a mobile phone, cracking real-estate deals and transmitting surf reports without ever leaving the beach. Bradshaw, who worked his way up as a Honolulu nightclub bouncer, denounced his 'lack of respect'. Foo was just a performer, a careerist, a glory-hunter.

January 18 1985 was a turning point. The Bay just kept on getting bigger.

Bradshaw, caught inside by a 30-footer, was forced to swim three times round the bay before making it in through the rip. Foo was the last guy out. He waved away a rescue helicopter and flew over the edge of a wave shaped like the sting of a scorpion. 'The unridden realm': that was Foo's attention-grabbing headline. After surviving the heaviest laundering of his career, he wrote up his 35ft wave – in an article that was syndicated around the world – as a 'date with destiny'. Bradshaw was caustic. 'Foo didn't actually ride the damn thing,' he snorted. It was just falling with style. Plus hype.

Bradshaw eventually turned to the outer reefs in search of bigger fish and Foo followed. They still differed in style and mentality, but the early

1990s saw a grudging rapprochement. When they took off together on the red-eye for San Francisco shortly before Christmas 1994, they shook hands on a merger: they would become a tow-in team and aim at waves far beyond the size attainable by paddling.

The next morning, at the newly discovered Mavericks, in northern California, brutal, cold and grey, Foo took off on a wave between 15 and 18ft. The mesmerising footage of his last moments at Mavericks shows him falling, then being dragged up the curtain, looped over, and then flung down and stomped on. Two hours later he was found dangling upside down in the water. Some – notably Foo's sister, SharLyn – blamed Bradshaw for giving scant attention to the 'buddy system'. Other said it was Foo's greatest ever publicity stunt. 'To die surfing a monster wave,' Foo once said, in a premonition of his own death, 'that would be the ultimate way to go.'

Foo's death was like a tombstone that marked the end of the classical period. He is still an 'honorary invitee' at the Quiksilver in Memory of Eddie Aikau big-wave contests, a celluloid idol, for ever at 36. Bradshaw doesn't get asked. But on January 28 1998 at Outside Log Cabins, Bradshaw towed into a wave estimated at more than 70ft (he says 80) that many reckon to be the biggest ever ridden.

The quest for a still larger wave, perhaps exceeding 100ft, continues.

Speaking as one who has yet to break through the 8ft barrier, I would like to suggest that, despite the current preoccupation with sheer volume of water, size is not everything. Passion and personality count, too. As one wise veteran once said: 'A wave is not measured in feet and inches; it is measured in increments of terror.'

Andy Martin

SIX

AIR

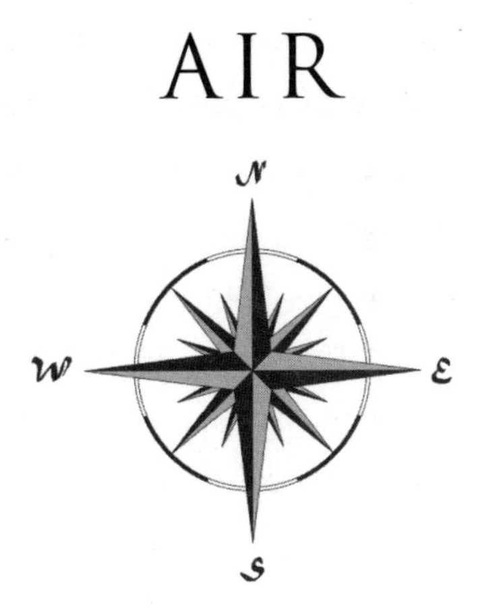

Blanchard, the aeronaut

Guardian, September 24 1845

The village of La Roche was, about 60 years since, the scene of an occurrence which sufficiently shows how isolated it was, and how completely ignorant its inhabitants were of what was then causing the liveliest sensation throughout the country. It was at the time when the discovery of aerostation had begun to excite attention, when Blanchard, the aeronaut – unworthy, however, as he appeared to be of the title of 'intrepid,' which has always been the property, de rigueur, of those who sail the skies – arrived at Liège. He obtained from the authorities permission to construct his balloon in the citadel, and establish a laboratory to supply him with the gas necessary for inflation. Everybody in the city and its neighbourhood impatiently waited the issue of an experiment fraught to them with so much novelty; and December 18 1786 was fixed upon for the ascent.

On the day appointed, the crowd to obtain admission to the citadel was so great, that a serious accident had nearly occurred, from the great pressure of the people anxious to secure the best places; it was, however, happily averted, and the numerous spectators, amongst whom were the prince bishop and all the municipal officers, were finally accommodated in safety. At a signal given by the discharge of artillery, the covering that concealed the balloon was all at once withdrawn, and the many-coloured orb appeared, held down to the earth, from which it seemed eager to escape, by a dozen men who grasped the cords. Blanchard was seated in the car. The immense machine was gently swayed over to where the prince was stationed, and Madame de Berlaiment, who sat beside him, descended from the platform, with a bouquet in her hand, which she presented to the aeronaut. Blanchard, affecting to stoop to receive it, desired the soldiers to cut the cords, and at the same time that the balloon flew up with rapidity of lighning, he quietly slid down to the ground, where he lay as if stunned by the fall. The prince rose in anger, and turning to those who sat near him, exclaimed, 'I was warned of the trick which this fellow intended to play us; but I could not believe that the impudent Frenchman would have audacity enough to sully his honour and reputation by an act offensive to a whole people.'

Then turning towards Blanchard, who still pretended to be in a swoon, 'I am not the dupe of your miserable jugglery,' he added, 'you shall not be lost sight of till you have constructed another balloon; and if you do not go up in it you shall be handed over to the arm of justice, and lose your head like a common robber.' Having uttered these words, he immediately got into his carriage, and returned to the palace. In the meantime the tenantless balloon soared majestically into the air, was for some time kept in view, and finally disappeared in the direction of the Ardennes.

Now it happened, sur ces entrefaites, that a great discussion had arisen in the little village of La Roche, in which piety and poverty were at issue. The images of the patron saint and the holy virgin were both in a pitiable condition as regarded costume, and the inhabitants were too poor to supply the wants of each; a collection was made, but it did not realise more than enough to purchase a robe for one. Opinions were divided, some declaring for the patron saint, others for Our Lady; the partisans of the former were in the majority, and on the day of his fete he appeared 'diaquant-neux,' in a garment of great splendour. But scarcely had his image received the honour due, when a wondrous object greeted the astonished eyes of the villagers, by the appearance in the sky of an enormous globe of resplendent hue, which descended directly upon the tower of the church. It was found on examination to be composed of silk, and the inhabitants of La Roche were at once convinced that it was a present from the virgin to deck her image! They acted immediately upon this impression, – the balloon was at once cut into pieces, and a series of robes was made that have honourably sustained the credit of the virgin's wardrobe from that day to this.

When I got into the valley between the castle and the opposite hill I found an eddying wind. I circled round twice to ease the descent, but I alighted heavier than I had anticipated, and the monoplane was damaged.

M. Blériot recently burned his foot severely through petrol escaping from the machine, and he is still lame in consequence. He is above the average height, and has the erect well-knit figure of an athlete. His attire for the flight consisted of a peculiarly made single brown combination garment in the style of a mechanic's overall, fitting very tightly over the limbs, and being continued over the neck and back of the head, which it closely fitted, covering also ears, chin and forehead, so that only the eyes, nose and lips were exposed to the tremendous wind which the aeroplane must have encountered in its rapid flight. When seated in the machine only M. Blériot's head and shoulders protruded. He was wearing a cork jacket beneath his overalls, and on the machine was a long India rubber cylinder filled with air, which would have acted as a float had any mishap occurred similar to Latham's.

The Great Britain air race

Guardian, July 25 1911

The 'Circuit of Great Britain' air race continued yesterday. Vedrines, the Frenchman, leaving Hendon just after four in the morning, reached Edinburgh at 25 seconds to eleven, having taken seven hours for the journey, including two stops. Beaumont reached Edinburgh shortly afterwards. Valentine arrived in Edinburgh a little after four o'clock in the afternoon. He had stopped four hours at Newcastle to repair his wings. These three

Hubert Latham flies into Blackpool in a gale, 1909

were the only competitors who completed the second stage. The rest of the 17 competitors either met with mishap yesterday or failed to start.

Shortly before ten o'clock Lieutenant Cammell came to grief near Castleford, West Riding. The cylinder of his engine blew out and dropped into some chemical works. He was compelled to descend. He planed down into a wheat field, and when near the ground his machine overturned.

Weymann descended near Leeds yesterday afternoon to inquire his way. On attempting to reascend he broke a wheel and had to return to earth. A crowd of nearly 20,000 people assembled in the field where the machine was stranded.

Pixton got within a few miles of Harrogate, but came down in the forenoon at Spofforth. With engine firing spasmodically, he flew directly over the village street, and was heard to be shouting, 'Where am I? Where's Harrogate?' After missing two or three obstacles his engine was heard to be sparking regularly, and the machine soared upwards. But the engine began to beat irregularly again, and after twice crossing the cricket field Pixton came down suddenly just short of the hedge.

Astley came to grief near Bedford. In a thick bank of cloud he imagined that he was riding at an altitude of a thousand feet or more. Instead he was only a few feet above the earth, and suddenly to his surprise he bumped upon a piece of rising ground, and his machine was damaged. Astley went on but a little later descended at Irthlingborough, having struck a gusty wind which tossed him about like a ship at sea. The rocking brought on sickness and he was unable to proceed.

Lieutenant Bier had a peculiar experience. The Austrian was carrying a passenger, and after a rapid journey from Hendon a defect in one of the cylinders developed, and a burst occurred, drenching the passenger with hot water. Bier had brought his aeroplane down suddenly into a cornfield from a height of 500 metres, and the landing was so abrupt that the lower part of the machine was smashed. The aviator decided to abandon the race.

Waiting for the airman

Guardian, May 30 1927

Croydon, Sunday evening: England is undoubtedly becoming air minded. When Sir John Alcock and Sir Arthur Whitten-Brown arrived in London after their flight from Newfoundland to Ireland in 1919 only a select few gathered to meet them. A fortnight ago a crowd of some 30,000 sought out the obscure village of Hamble, in Hampshire, to witness an air display. And today a vast throng, roughly estimated at 100,000, made their way to the somewhat inaccessible aerodrome at Croydon to catch a glimpse, if possible, of the daring young American pilot [who had flown across the Atlantic to Paris single handed].

It was by far the biggest crowd which has ever assembled at Croydon aerodrome, and the confines of the aerodrome did not contain all the worshippers. On every point of vantage in the neighbourhood throngs were gathered together. The officials of Imperial Airways were distinctly apprehensive a good hour before the arrival as they saw the palings bending under the gentle pressure of a multitude which was still waiting with the phlegmatic patience of the Londoner. A clear landing space was especially desirable because in the Ryan monoplane the pilot is completely enclosed in the fuselage and can only see around by means of periscopes.

Captain Lindbergh, however, is not as other men are. The *Spirit of St Louis* does not carry wireless; so, in order that Captain Lindbergh's progress might be duly reported, one of the Imperial Airways pilots, Captin Mackintosh, in a DH50, whch is equipped with wireless, had crossed over to Brussels and flew back with him, talking to Croydon as they flew. Four Handley Page liners, three of them with twin Napier Lions and one with three Jupiter engines, also proceeded towards the coast to escort the hero of the hour into London's airport. Private machines, Avros, Moths, etc, also went up in considerable numbers, and circled round the aerodrome. The pleasure flight Avros were very busy, and though one of them came down rather hard in an adjoining field and did some damage to itself, the passengers were little the worse, and the mishap did not deter the stream of applicants for flights.

Several hours before Captain Lindbergh was due to leave Brussels people began to flock to the Croydon airport. Arrangements had been made to accommodate upwaards of 100,000 spectators, but so keen was the desire to secure an advantageous spot from which to witness the arrival of Captain Lindbergh and his escort of planes that some enthusiasts arrived during the early morning, armed with luncheon baskets.

At 5.52 the klaxon horn in the control tower gave raucous warning that a machine was coming in to land, and soon, to the left of the Crystal Palace, we could discern a number of black dots in the sky. As they grew larger we could see three large biplanes abreast, three other biplanes to the rear, while between the two lines was a tiny dot of a monoplane.

The aeroplanes flew in low over our heads and circled round. The monoplane dipped in a salute to acknowledge this wonderful welcome from Great Britain, and immediately went up in a steep climb. This was repeated three or four times, and the flying experts all admired the clean lines of the machine and the way in which the pilot handled it. At last Lindbergh shut off his engine and glided down to land. His wheels touched the earth, but he had come down rather fast and he bumped up two or three times. By this time the barriers had collapsed and the crowd was beginning to stream across the landing ground. Perhaps the pilot in his cabin was not sure that his way was clear, for he opened up his engine, flew round again, and then finally landed.

Captain Lindbergh was taken to the control tower and showed himself from the balcony which runs round it. He said a few words to the crowd through a megaphone. I think he merely said, 'Than you all very much. What can I say better?'

Major FA de V Robertson

Amy Johnson, the tyro pilot who flew to Australia

Guardian, May 24 1930

It is not really the sex of the pilot so much as her comparative inexperience which makes this flight of Amy Johnson so remarkable. She made her first solo flight on June 9 last year, and took her A licence at the end of the same month. Before starting for Australia she put in less than ninety hours in the air. She had only made one considerable cross-country flight – from London to her home at Hull. England is well provided with railway lines, towns and all the other features which simplify the task of navigation in the air. This experience was very scant equipment for a flight to Australia. Yet Miss Johnson acutally beat Hinkler's time to India. He had his bad luck in North Africa; hers came later in Burma and the Dutch East Indies.

Hinkler's record to Australia in a light aeroplane still stands, but Miss Johnson's flight to India was a marvellous performance. Safety first is a rule which is generally accepted on all regular travel routes, including regular airways, but the time has not yet come when private pilots will accept it. When that time does come, it will be admitted that the crossing of the Timor Sea from the East Indies to Darwin ought not to be attempted in a land plane with no reserve engine. Sir Ross Smith's Vimy had two engines, but needed them both, and before the Vimy started off across the Timor Sea the party inflated all their spare tyres to serve as lifebelts. By the time an aeroplane has reached Bima both macihne and engine are probably somewhat worn, and the pilot is bound to be suffering from strain. These factors increase the risk which, even without them, is certainly not justifiable.

Major FA de V Robertson

To the moon and beyond

Guardian, January 5 1959

There will be unstinted admiration, not to say astonishment, for what the Russians have done with their rocket to the moon. By all reasonable tests it has been an unqualified success. Since there was no possibility that the rocket could have been captured into an orbit around the moon – this would have required some means of slowing it down early yesterday morning – it is just as well that it has not hit the surface and disturbed the dust on the crater floors. It is far better that the rocket should travel on, collecting information and relaying it back to Earth as long as its batteries last.

After all, its approach to the moon was as near a miss as anyone could expect or even wish. Quite properly the Americans were saying last autumn that they would be content if their rockets got within 50,000 miles of the moon; such is the precision needed to aim a rocket through the Earth's gravitational field where it must be continually robbed of headway. Now it is clear, as the regularity of the Sputnik launchings suggested, that the Russians are masters of the accurate guidance of rockets off the ground.

For scientific purposes a miss of less than 5,000 miles is hardly a miss at all. But what comes next? Obviously the Russian rocket is not the last in the field. Even if the Russians were content, the Americans will now feel bound to show that they can do better. The corridors of Washington will again be ringing with talk of 'crash programmes', as they were when the first Sputnik went up. There will be more rockets which do much the same as the Russian rocket, and very soon there will be rockets that make a landing on the moon and rockets that reach out to Mars and Venus. It will not be much more than a decade before someone – now probably a boy at school – is eventually persuaded to put his life in the hands of the rocket and electronics engineers.

We have to recognise now that the exploration of space (at least within the solar system) by rocket instrument and by human senses is feasible. Whether or not it is desirable is a matter for the individual's choice and for the national treasuries.

Leader

Russia hails 'Columbus of space'

Guardian, April 13 1961

Major Yuri Alexeyevitch Gagarin, the world's first astronaut, was last night undergoing a rigorous medical examination to find out the effects on him of his journey yesterday in orbit round the world in the Soviet space ship Vostok. 'The Columbus of interplanetary space,' as Moscow Radio described him, is expected to reach Moscow tomorrow where a hero's welcome is being prepared for him. Major Gagarin, aged 27, a member of the Red Air Force, is a married man with two young daughters.

Early yesterday morning his space ship, weighing more than four and a half tons without its last-stage rocket, went into orbit at 18,000 mph, made rather more than one complete circuit of the earth, and landed safely at a prearranged area 108 minutes later. The Russian places where he left and landed were not disclosed. Mr Khrushchev, according to Tass, told him by telephone: 'You have brought glory to our homeland. You have shown courage and heroism. You have made yourself immortal … I shall be glad to meet you in Moscow. I, together with you and all our people, will solemnly celebrate this great feat.' The Major reported he was 'well, with no injuries'. Meanwhile in Moscow, to martial music broadcast by loudspeakers, crowds were filling the streets, some singing and chanting 'To the cosmos,' in a burst of enthusiasm that was said to have been the greatest seen in the capital for many years.

Mr Macmillan and President Kennedy yesterday led the world in hailing Russia's success. In Ottawa, the British prime minister described the orbiting as 'a very notable achievement', and added that he was sending a message of congratulations to Mr Khrushchev. President Kennedy told a press conference that the flight was 'a most impressive scientific accomplishment.'

He had sent a message to Mr Khrushchev, saying: 'The people of the US share with the people of the Soviet Union their satisfaction for the safe flight of the astronaut in man's first venture into space … It is my sincere desire that in the continuing quest for knowledge of outer space our nations can work together to obtain the greatest benefit to mankind.'

He said of the relative positions of the US and Russia in space exploration that there was no doubt that 'we are behind'. But the latest Soviet feat did not mean the free world was losing the world contest with communism.

Gagarin burst out singing for joy

Guardian, April 14 1961

Moscow, April 13: Major Yuri Gagarin described today how it felt to be the first man in space – how he was able to write and work and how he burst out singing for joy as his ship plunged back towards the earth. 'Everything was easier to perform ... legs and arms weighed nothing,' he told a Soviet interviewer. Objects swam about in the cabin and he actually sat suspended above his chair in mid-air, gazing out in admiration at the beauty of the earth floating in a black sky.

'I ate and drank and everything was like on earth,' he went on. 'My handwriting did not change, though the hand was weightless. But it was necessary to hold the writing block as otherwise it would float away from the hands ...' The passage from weightlessness to gravitation was gradual and smooth as he descended. He had wanted to be a space traveller. 'The wish to fly in space was my own personal wish. When I was given this task, I began to prepare for the flight, and as you see, my wish has come true.'

Describing his feelings during the flight, Major Gagarin said: 'I was entirely concentrated on carrying out the flight programme. I wanted to carry out every point of the assignment and to do it as well as possible. There was a lot of work. The entire flight meant work.' ... Describing how the earth looks from space, he said: 'The sunlit side of the earth is visible quite well, and one can easily distinguish the shores of continents, islands, great rivers, large areas of water, and folds of the land.' Flying over Soviet territory he saw distinctly the great squares of the fields of collective farms, and could tell what was ploughland and what was meadowland.

'Before this I had never been above 15,000 metres (49,213 feet). From the spaceship satellite one does not, of course, see as well as from an aeroplane, but very, very well all the same. During the flight I saw for the first time with my own eyes the earth's spherical shape. You can see its curvature when looking to the horizon.

'I must say the view of the horizon is quite unique and very beautiful. It is possible to see the remarkably colourful change from the light surface of the earth to the completely black sky in which one can see the stars. This dividing line is very thin, just like a belt of film surrounding the earth's sphere. It is of a delicate blue colour. And this transition from the blue to the dark is very gradual and lovely. It is difficult to put it in words. When I emerged from the shadow of the earth the horizon looked different. There was a bright orange strip along it, which again passed into a blue hue and once again into a dense black colour.

I did not see the moon. The sun in outer space is tens of times brighter than here on earth. The stars are visible very well: they are bright and distinct. The whole picture of the heavens is much more contrasty than when seen from the earth.'

'One small step for a man, but one giant leap for mankind'

Guardian, July 21 1969

Neil Armstrong, the Apollo 22 commander, crawled feet first out of the lunar module's hatch shortly before 4am today and climbed down a ladder to become the first man to set foot on the moon. 'OK, Houston, I am on the pad,' he said at 3.56am as he stepped down on to the lunar module's extended leg. He described the lunar soil as like powdered charcoal and said that his boots went in about an eighth-of-an-inch.

'This is one small step for a man,' he said as he stepped from the lunar module on to the moon, 'but one giant leap for mankind.'

He reported finding no difficulty in moving about in the moon's gravity, one sixth of that on earth. Half way down the ladder he pulled a lever to deploy the television camera that recorded his first historic step on to the surface. As the television pictures came on at the Space Centre in Houston a wild cheer went up from press correspondents gathered watching the monitor screen and in the flight control room we could see hands flying up with people congratulating one another.

After getting his balance, Armstrong's first action was to gather a sample of soil with a large scoop rather like a butterfly net to be stowed into a hip pocket in case he had to make a rapid return to lunar module, *Eagle*. Shortly after this he was joined on the surface by Edwin Aldrin. As Aldrin backed out of the hatch, guided by directions from Armstrong, he joked: 'I'm making certain not to lock it.' On sliding down the last three feet to the surface he almost seemed to jump for joy in the one sixth gravity. 'Isn't that something!' he said as he bounced up and down.

The black and white television gave superb pictures of both Armstrong and Aldrin gliding and hopping round the lunar module almost like kangaroos. Aldrin said: 'I can bend down easily. I can also reach up. It really seems easy.' Earlier, the lunar module had landed in a wide, rocky plan four miles down range from the target area in the Sea of Tranquillity. 'Tranquillity Base here. The *Eagle* has landed,' said Armstrong, a man with a just reputation for saying little.

The astronauts were not certain where they had come down because their landmark tracking in the final approach was interrupted by alarms in the lunar module's cabin. Ground tracking stations initially estimated their position as 0.799 degrees North, 26 degrees East, near the lunar equator, well outside the planned landing area. Mr Gene Kranz, flight director, said last night that the alarms were caused by computers in the lunar module becoming over-loaded. It was still not known, he said, why *Eagle* had missed the target area by four miles.

Armstrong described the scene out of his small triangular window shortly after landing: 'It seems to be a relatively level plain with a fairly large number of craters of the 5ft to 50ft variety and some ridges, mostly small but some 20ft to 60ft high, and literally thousands of little 1ft and 2ft high craters around the area.

'We see some angular blocks several hundred feet in front of us that are perhaps 2ft. in size and have angular edges.'

Armstrong said the rocks were mainly grey in colour but Aldrin noted it depended on which way you looked: 'There is about every variety of rocks you can find,' he said. 'The colour depends on which way you look but there doesn't appear to be much of a general colour at all.'

The landing manoeuvres began shortly after 6.40pm (BST) last night when Armstrong, standing on the left of Aldrin in the lunar module, released the docking latches and *Eagle* backed slowly away from Columbia, the command module. Collins, the command module pilot, then took a close look from about 40 feet at the lunar module as it revolved slowly, reporting that its landing gear was fully extended. 'Looks like you have a fine flying machine there,' he said. After this pirouetting for inspection, Columbia thrust away for 2,000 feet. In the control-room at Houston there was electric tension as controllers anxiously monitored the displays in front of them. Step by step the unemotional voices of ground control transmitted orders to *Eagle* and back came equally calm responses. Shortly before 8pm flight control said: 'You are go for DOI (descent orbit insertion).' Back came the single syllable answer from the spacecraft through a mass of static: 'Rog.' Eight minutes later, at 8.06pm, the descent to the moon began.

The engine fired on 10 per cent throttle for the first 15 seconds, gradually increasing to 40 per cent, putting *Eagle* into a highly elliptical orbit with a low point of only 50,000 feet above the moon's surface. Then, with Aldrin and Armstrong standing side by side in the lunar module the descent engine was refired by computer command, breaking the orbital speed for the final 230 miles on a slanting course to the moon.

Eight minutes after the descent engine fired *Eagle* was barely 7,500 feet above the surface, and it then swung to a nearly vertical position to allow the astronauts to peer out of the triangular windows in front of them at the approaching Sea of Tranquillity.

Ninety seconds later, with the spacecraft flying at about 45 mph forward and 10 mph downward, Aldrin took over manual control from

Eagle's computer. For the last 150 feet he held the lunar module in a hovering position directly above the landing site and then very slowly throttled back the engine until the probes touched the moon surface. There was a delay of one second. The engines were cut, and the lunar module jolted on to the moon.

Adam Raphael, at the Space Centre, Houston

The compulsive adventurer

Guardian, July 21 1969

No other great adventure was as great as this. The human race can manage anything (except its own affairs) and two quiet Americans are on the moon to prove it. We have been looking curiously at the moon for a million years and now we are there and all the science fiction writers have proved their point. Man had to get there because man is a compulsive discoverer. Curiosity is the begetter of great adventures and the common quality in all adventurers. Armstrong and Aldrin are supremely competent navigators and so was Columbus, by the standards of his time, but what they all needed as well as competence was the determination to find out for themselves. Columbus did not know America was there. Before they landed Armstrong and Aldrin did not know for sure that the moon's surface would support their spacecraft. They still do not know for sure whether they can ascend again. They are there to find out.

Man's landing on the moon is not just supreme technology, it is adventure too. President Kennedy wanted an American on the moon and he wanted the American to be there first. Kennedy's motives were not primarily scientific or even, perhaps, adventurous. He felt that the United States was competing in space against Russia and that the United States must win. The people of the United States have since spent vast sums and have harnessed the energies of thousands of their best engineers and pilots and they have won. To divert all this treasure from other projects may be counted serious mismanagement of the world's resources, but the diversion was inevitable. Kennedy's motives may have been questionable. But someone was going to the moon and was surely going to get there long before hunger had been conquered in Asia or civil rights had been restored in Alabama.

No doubt the money, effort, and skill that has been spent on the moon landing could have been used in other ways which would have done mankind far more good. The scientists, left to themselves, might not have advised spending so much on such a limited project. We do not know whether the samples that Armstrong and Aldrin are collecting today will tell astronomers or others very much that they need to know. And as the Russians have been saying a machine can collect samples too.

Yet even the most sceptical scientists have to concede that no remote-controlled machine can match the discriminating judgment of a man who sets foot on the moon, and decides for himself what sample of rock to bring back to earth, or where precisely to mount the instruments he leaves on the moon. The scientific value of the moon landing may be questioned, but it is as a human achievement that it must be judged. July 20 marks the day when man showed that he can step outside the gravity–bound limits of earth. That is what makes it a watershed in human history.

Leader

A 'nice evening' – then the Apollo crisis

Guardian, April 15 1970

A few minutes before the Apollo-13 emergency, Captain James Lovell, the commander of the spacecraft, had wished his television audience on earth a 'nice evening'. With this crew – Fred Haise and Jack Swigert – he looked forward to a 'pleasant evening' aboard the command module, Odyssey. Five minutes after the television tour of the inside of the moon landing craft, Aquarius, the spacemen heard a bang and Lovell said: Hey, we've got a problem here.

Mission control (Houston): Say again, please

Lovell: Houston, we've had a problem. We've had a main BUS interval (a fault in the electrical power system).

Lovell reported an oxygen gauge reading zero and the spacecraft began to gyrate.

'Why the hell are we manouvering?' Haise demanded. 'I can't take that doggone roll out,' Lovell observed as he tried to fire control thrusters to stop the gyrations.

The fault had not looked too serious at first, and Haise had said: Right now, Houston, the voltage is looking good. We had a pretty large bang associated with the caution and warning alarm system.

One of the astronauts then said something was 'venting' from the spacecraft – a 'gas' of some sort.' The seriousness of the situation soon became evident, and there were rapid exchanges of technical jargon between the spacecraft and ground control.

Houston: Can you tell us anything about the venting; where is it coming from; what window do you see it at?

Spacecraft: It's coming out of window one right now.

When the Apollo crew began to complain about the pitch and roll, Houston assured them that 'lots of people' were working on their problem. 'We'll get some dope as soon as we have it, and you'll be the first to know,' they were told.

Houston was thanked for the assurance, and almost immediately afterwards one of the crew reported that an electric distribution box was 'killed completely ... it's dead.'

The failure which jeopardized Apollo-13 was in the service module, not Odyssey or Aquarius. But it caused Odyssey to lose all electric power. This meant that its computers, life-support systems, instruments and lights all had to be switched off. Oxygen used for breathing and power for some of the spaceship's systems had leaked from a tank in the service module.

As instruments in the spacecraft and on the ground confirmed the extent of the trouble, Houston said: We're starting to think about the LM lifeboat (a reference to Aquarius).

Spacecraft: Yes, that's something we're thinking about, too.

Shortly afterwards, Houston told the spacecraft: We figure we'll get about 15 minutes worth of power left in the command module (Odyssey). So we want you to start getting over in the lunar module (Aquarius) and get some power on that. Are you ready to copy your procedure?

Spacecraft: Okay.

Houston: We'd like you to start making your way over to the lunar module now.

Swigert: Fred and Him (Haise and Lovell) are in the LM.

Houston: Okay, Jack. Thank you.

Swigert: I got LM power on. Okay. You still with us, Houston? Okay, Houston, are you reading 13 (Apollo)?

Houston: Reading you loud and clear, Jack.

Throughout the height of the crisis, Captain Lovell and his crew remained cool, almost laconic, while the orders transmitted from the ground were crisp and businesslike. There was one rare moment of informality. Jack Swigert, who replaced the astronaut who had been exposed to German measles, told ground control: I want to say you guys are doing real good work.

And the informal reply from Houston: 'So are you, Jack.'

The first man on the moon

Guardian, July 2 2009

Even at the time, we understood that our world had changed and that we could pinpoint this change to almost the second. We didn't have to wait for Neil Armstrong to get out of the lunar module and fumble a portentous remark about a small step for a man. When we heard the words 'Houston, Tranquillity Base here, the *Eagle* has landed,' it didn't quite sink in, but then after a short, eerie pause the man at Houston, known only as Capcom, choked a bit and stumbled and then said: 'We copy you on the ground. You've got a bunch of guys about to turn blue. We're breathing again.' That was the moment a hundred million people around the world also started breathing again.

Apollo was momentous in a way that Yuri Gagarin's first, heroic orbit could never have been. Gagarin had circled the Earth in 92 minutes in 1961. He had travelled 24,000 miles in an hour and a half; he had made history; he had confirmed Soviet space supremacy; he had done a thing that many thought could never be done. But two things separated him from the Apollo team eight years later. One was that Gagarin had done all these things before anyone in the world knew about them, or could have known about them. We cheered his triumph, but missed the drama. The other was that he never really left the Earth; he flew higher than anybody had ever done, but he was still a prisoner of the planet's tug. He was never much further from Earth than Manchester is from London.

Everything about the Apollo landing, though, was high adventure. It was the climax of a space race that had been so tightly contested that, right up to that moment on the Sea of Tranquillity, it had seemed possible that the Russians might get there first. This race had developed, although we could not know the details at the time, from a duel of wits between two men. One was Wernher von Braun, the former Waffen-SS officer who had devised, built, tested and deployed what, in 1944, had been the ultimate weapon: the Vergeltungswaffe-2, the vengeance weapon, the V2 . He pioneered the American technocracy. His Soviet opponent was a figure so shadowy that even in the USSR he was known only as 'the Chief Designer'. In fact, Sergei Kolorev was an even more remarkable man who had lost his teeth, his health and very nearly his life in Stalin's prison camps, but most of us knew nothing about him, not even his name, until 1990.

We forget this now, but in 1969, the fear of global infection by alien lunar organisms seemed real enough to ensure that the three astronauts went straight into biological isolation when they came home. Above all, it was a moment of human drama, played out with fragile, gleaming technology against a backcloth of infinity. Like a billion other people, I listened, on an old junkshop radio with an improvised antenna, in the small parlour of a two-up, two-down railwayman's cottage in Kent, while my wife, son and daughter slept overhead. I wasn't, at the time, a science reporter, but I had joined a newspaper at 16 in 1957, just in time for Sputnik 1 and, like millions of others, I had followed every step of the drama that, on the night of July 20 1969, reached its highest point.

Neil Armstrong, Buzz Aldrin and Mike Collins had left the Earth altogether. They had travelled a quarter of a million miles, and then two of them had climbed into a little module that looked then, and still looks now, implausible, and descended to leave their footprints in the dust of an alien world, and they did these things while almost the whole of the human race watched and listened and, yes, held its breath. *Eagle*'s touchdown on the moon was the unforgettable moment: one in which we might eavesdrop on triumph or tragedy. We knew that astronauts could get out of a spacecraft and walk in space; it would be no problem to get out and walk on the moon. That much was a formality, a performance for the cameras they carried with them.

What was not certain was that the *Eagle* could land at all. Consider the problem: *Eagle* had to detach itself from the mothership Apollo at the right moment, and begin a precise descent that had to be completed while still on the side of the moon always facing Earth: radio transmission was impossible from the far side. Although Aldrin and Armstrong were astronauts, test pilots and history-makers, they were also the agents of the most ambitious peacetime co-operative enterprise ever: they were emissaries from Earth, touching down on another world. They were part of a corporate journey into the unknown that could go terribly wrong at any point, and they had to do it while mission control at Houston could monitor the technology, and while the world watched.

'Apollo 11 was a half-a-million-mile daisy chain draped around the moon, a chain that was as fragile as it was long,' Collins wrote afterwards. 'I figured our chances for a successful landing and return were not much better than 50-50.' Nasa's safety chief during the Apollo 8 mission, the one that flew round the moon in 1968, had calculated that the spaceship had 5,600,000 moving parts and 'even if all functioned with 99.9% reliability, we could expect 5,600 defects'.

But how much more potentially calamitous was the flight of the *Eagle*, the module that landed on the moon. There were no circumstances in which anyone could really complete a test flight of the ungainly little vehicle with its ridiculous legs. You could not simulate lunar gravity on Earth; you could not simulate a 60-mile journey in a vacuum anywhere here; and you could not mock-up the fine detail of a lunar surface – the dust, stones, boulders, crags, crevices, chasms and craters – because until the touchdown, nobody had ever seen the fine detail. Could *Eagle* find a level surface? Or might it land on a slope, on unstable ground, on a protruding rock, and topple over, so much expensive wreckage on a hostile shore? And even if it could land safely upright, might it not sink into the dust, to be trapped in lunar quicksand, never to escape?

In the 1960s, the world marvelled at Nasa's state-of-the-art computers, but one forgets how new this art was. Any household washing machine now has greater memory, more sophisticated programming and faster processing power than the entire sum of Nasa's computing resources at the time. Like Captain Cook and other 18th-century mariners before them, the astronauts had to back up their computer-guided navigation system by making star sightings with a sextant. Essentially, the whole $24bn operation rested on Newtonian mechanics, slide-rule mathematics, the watchfulness of 60,000 Nasa chiefs, scientists and engineers, and the labour of 400,000 men and women employed by 20,000 private contractors.

When it reached the moon, the mother ship had to go into a precise circular orbit around the new world, because Armstrong and Aldrin had to take their little lifeboat down there and then back again. It was one thing to touch down on the moon – they could hardly miss. But it would be quite another thing to take off in what was little more than a tent wrapped in foil and perched on stilts, and make a rendezvous with something the size of a small caravan moving at thousands of miles an hour. So everything had to go right. And of course, things went wrong. The alarm systems on board *Eagle* started complaining as it began its descent: engineers and mission controllers and the astronauts themselves had to make a terrible calculation. Was it just the warning technology playing up, or was there something really wrong? Should they abort? And could they successfully abort?

Collins, the man who stayed behind aboard Apollo, whirling round and round the moon, had a checklist of 18 different rescue scenarios clipped to his pressure suit, in case things went wrong. Some of these had to be executed immediately, and flawlessly, to avert tragedy. Collins, too, while waiting for the touchdown, the moon walk, the show for an estimated billion television viewers, and the take-off, had more time than the others to think about things that might go wrong. If the ascent engine wouldn't fire, then Armstrong and Aldrin would be marooned with just a day's supply of oxygen. 'How would Nasa handle that? Would Nasa pull the plug or keep broadcasting their final words to the world? What would I say or do?' he wrote years later in his memoir *Liftoff*.

The duo made it safely, in a cliff-hanger landing. They also began their two and a half hour extra-vehicular activity (EVA) and stepped from *Eagle* to the dust of the moon seven hours earlier than planned, because, as Aldrin put it in his book *Men from Earth*, 'Whoever signed off on that plan didn't know much psychology … Telling us to try to sleep before the EVA was like telling kids on Christmas morning they had to stay in bed till noon.' They stepped down, Armstrong said the bit that everybody in the world can quote, and then he said what he really felt: he turned to Aldrin and said: 'Isn't that something?' What followed happened according to a script already arranged, with an awkward few minutes of improvisation when President Nixon telephoned from the White House: 'Neil and Buzz … this certainly has to be the most historic telephone call ever made.' The pair planted a flag and left a plaque ('We came in peace …') and a medal in memory of Yuri Gagarin.

They walked no more than 60 metres from the lander, gathered 40lb of moon rocks, and set up two experiments, one of which failed in the harsh lunar climate and one of which worked for 40 years. After that they prepared for the return journey. It was then that they discovered something that very few others knew about at the time: one of them, in turning inside the lunar module while wearing the oxygen pack and helmet, had snapped off a little plastic circuit breaker. It was the circuit that would send electrical power to the engine to fire the rockets that would get them off the moon. Both men were by this time suffering from severe fatigue – they had barely slept at all in 36 hours – but, as Aldrin put it afterwards, 'this got our attention'. They shoved a felt-tip pen into the slot, and luckily, it fitted. They consulted mission control, began the countdown and took off. This time everything went right: four hours later, they had docked with Apollo.

A few days later Senator Teddy Kennedy, brother of the late John Kennedy, was trying to explain the mysterious death of a girl off a bridge at Chappaquiddick, Nixon was talking again about the war in Vietnam and Britain abolished the halfpenny. Somehow, we were back to business as usual.

A new era was to begin: there would one day be huge satellite cities in space, colonies on the moon, an outpost on Mars, and all before 2001.

Tim Radford

REFERENCES

Allen, Benedict (ed) *The Faber Book of Exploration* (Faber and Faber, 2002)

Anderson, JRL *The Ulysses Factor* (Harcourt Brace Jovanovich, 1970)

Bonington, Chris *Quest for Adventure* (Hodder and Stoughton, 1981)

Ferguson, Niall *Empire: How Britain Made the Modern World* (Allen Lane, 2003)

Fleming, Fergus *Tales of Endurance* (Wiedenfeld & Nicolson, 2004)

Huntford, Roland *Two Planks and a Passion* (Continuum, 2008)

Lunn, Arnold *A Century of Mountaineering 1857-1957* (George Allen and Unwin, 1957)

Murray, Nicholas *A Corkscrew is Most Useful* (Little, Brown, 2008)

Nelsson, Richard (ed) *The Guardian Book of Mountains* (guardianbooks, 2007)

Powter, Geoff *We Cannot Fail* (Robinson, 2007)

Riffenburgh, Beau *The Myth of the Explorer* (John Wiley and Sons, 1993)

Spufford, Francis *I May Be Some Time* (Faber and Faber, 1996)

Taylor, Geoffrey *Changing Faces: A History of the Guardian, 1956-88* (Fourth Estate, 1993)

The Guardian and Observer digital archive: archive.guardian.co.uk

The Guardian News & Media archive: guardian.co.uk/gnm-archive

INDEX

Adelaide, 57
Adelie Land, 28
Aden, Yemen, 74
Advent Bay, Svalbard 20
Afghanistan, 165
Africa, 115, 116, 117, 126, 208
  See also West Africa
Aikau, Eddie 212
Alaska, 50, 122
Alcock, Sir John, 222
  Flight Newfoundland to
    Ireland of 1919, 222
Aldrin, 'Buzz' Edwin, 2, 4, 6
    231-235, 240, 242-244
Aleppo, Syria 62, 63, 64
Algeria, 65, 77, 80
Allen, Benedict, 127-130
Alps, 157
Amazon Jungle, 130, 131
  See also Amazon Rainforest
Amazon Rainforest, 130, 131
  See also Amazon Jungle
Amedeo, Luigi, Duke of the
    Abruzzi, 138
America, 9, 38, 96, 200
  See also United States
Amundsen, Roald, 2, 21, 25,
    36, 39, 49
  1911 expedition, 21-25
  Scott and Amundsen, Roland
    Huntford, 42-44
Andes, 142-144
  Plane crash survival, 171-173
Anderson, JRL, 47
  The Ulysses Factor, 47-48
  Vinland Voyage, 200-202
  High Mountains and Cold Seas: A Biography of HW Tilman
    208-210
Andrée, Salomon August, 38
  Arctic balloon expedition of
    1897, 38
Angkor, Cambodia, 94, 95
Antarctic, 28, 30, 39, 48, 52
  Hope Bay station, 49
  Herbert Plateau, 49
  Queen Maud Mountains, 49
  Beardmore glacier, 49
  Transantarctic Mountains,
    49
Antarctic Plateau, 24
  See also King Haakon VII
    Plateau
Apollo 13 Emergency 1970,
    236-238
Apollo-22 Space Mission,
    230-235
Arabian Desert, 68, 77, 81
Arctic, 48, 51, 52
  Salomon August Andree
    balloon expedition, 1897,
    38
Arctic Ocean, 51
Armenia, 113
Amstrong, Neil 2, 4, 6, 230,
    235, 238, 240, 242-244
  Apollo-22 Space Mission
    1969, 230-235
  The Eagle lunar module, 231,
    232, 233, 240, 241
Asia, 9
Astley, HJD, 212
Atlantic, 191, 195
  First rowing of the Atlantic
    1896, 196-199
  Record attempt 1966,
    196-199
  English Rose III, 196-199
  Hurricane Alma, 198
Audouin-Dubreuil, Lieutenant
    Louis, 66
  1923 French expedition by
    car, 65-67
Austin, Marv, 119
Australia, 57- 60, 86, 111
Axel Heibergs glacier, 22, 49

Back, Sir George, 13
Back River, 13
  See also Great Fish River
Baffin Bay, 8
Baffin, William, 8
Baghdad, 61, 63, 113
Baker, Sir Samuel, 125-127
  The Albert N'Yanza, 125
Balmat, Jacques, 133-135
Band, George, 169
Barber, Noel, 41, 42
  The White Desert, 41
Bathysphere 185-188
  Bathyscaphe *Trieste* 192-194
Beaumont, Andre, 220
Beaverbrook, Lord William
    Maxwell Aitken, 82
Bedouin, the 69, 77, 78
Behring Strait, 9
Bell, Gertrude Lowthian,
    60-65
  Amurath to Amurath, 60-65
Beebe, Dr William 185-188
  Bathysphere 185-188
Bember, Lake, Zambia 117
Benin, Republic of , 90
  See also Dahomey
Bier, Lieutenant, 212
Bioko, 96
  See also Fernando Po,
    Equatorial Guinea
Bishop, Isabella 110- 115
Blake, Sir Peter, 211
Blanc, Mont 133-135
  First ascent 1786, 133-135
  Glacier de Bosson, 134
  Dome du Goute, 134
  Joseph Brown, 1954
    expedition, 168
  Clyth, Segeant Chay
    196-199
Blanchard, Jean-Pierre,
    215-217
  Aeronaut 'flight' of 1786,
    216
Blériot, Louis 4, 218-220
  Monoplane flight across the
    English Channel, 218-220
Bombard, Dr Alain 191-192
  The Bombard Story, 191-192
Borneo, 99

Bosphorous, 61
 See also Istanbul Strait
Bradshaw, Ken, 212-213
Britain, 42, 90
British Antarctic Survey, 48
 See also Falkland Islands
  Dependencies Survey, 48
British Consul, 55
British Empire, 125
Brooke, James, 99
 See also Rajah Brooke
Brown, Joseph, 166-170
 Himalayan Expedition,
  1955, 167
 Pennines, 167
 Mont Blanc, 1954, 168
 Kanchenjunga conquest, 169
Burney, James, 9
Burton, Sir Richard F., 76, 87,
  109, 125
 A Mission to Gelele, King of
  Dahome, 95-99
Burton, Isabel, 88, 89

Cable, Mildred, 67
 Gobi Desert expedition,
  1927, 67-71
Caird Coast, 29
Calabar River, West Africa
  108
Cambodia, 94, 95
Cammell, Lieutenant, 221
Cameroon, Mount, 109
Cape Fligely, 15
Cape of Good Hope, 9
Castelnau, Paul, 66
Central Mount Stuart, 59
Chalmers Adams, Harriet, 119
Chambezi, River, 107
Cherry-Garrard, Apsley, 44
Chesney, Colonel Francis
  Rawdon, 61
Chichester, Francis 194-196,
  203, 205
 Plymouth to New York solo
  passage, 194-196
China, 67, 68, 73, 111, 114
 Great Wall, 68
Christian, 56, 62, 64, 74, 84
Collins, Barry 174
 The Ice Chimney, 174
Collins, Mike, 240, 242

Cochinchina, Vietnam 94
Constantinople, 63
Conway, Sir Martin, 17, 18,
  19, 20
 The Bolivian Andes, 142-144
Cook, Frederick, 50, 52
Cook, Captain James, 2
Crean, Tom, 34, 35
Cromer, Lord Evelyn Baring,
  61
Crowhurst, Donald 203-207
 Sunday Times Golden Globe
  Race hoax, 203-207

d'Arlandes, Francois Laurent,
  3
Dahomey, 90, 95-99
 See also *Republic of Benin*
 King Gelele of Dahomey,
  95-99
Damascus, 89
Danakil Desert, 76
Darwin, Charles, 3, 100, 101
David-Neel, Alexandra
  151-152
 My Journey to Lhasa, 151-152
Davidson, Robyn, 86, 87
 Gibson Desert Expedition,
  86-87
Dayak, the 102
 See also Dyak
Deir ez-Zor, 63
Desjoyeaux, Michel, 210,
  211
Devil's glacier, 23
Dinka, the 76
Dolomites, 178
Don Pedro Christophersens
  Mountain, 23
Doughty, Charles Montagu
  76, 77, 81-86
 Travels in Arabia Deserta, 82
Douglas, Lord Francis,
  135-138
Dyak, The 102
 See also Dayak

Easter Island, 188
Egypt, 48, 80, 81
Eiger, The, 156
 See also *Alps*
 1935 Expedition, 157-159

Elephant Island, 29, 33
Elias, Mount, 122
Ellsmere Island, 50
Emerson, Gertrude, 119
Empty Quarter 68, 69, 76, 77,
  78, 79
 See also Rub' al Khali
English Channel, 183-185
 First flight over 218-220
Ethiopia, 76
Everest, Mount, 148, 150-151,
  153, 161, 174, 180
 Mallory Expedition, 1924,
  150-151
 Nanda Devi, 154, 155

Falklands Islands, 48
 Falklands Islands
  Dependencies Survey, 48
 See also British Antarctic
  Survey
Fawcett, Colonel Percy,
  121-125, 130-132
Fernando Po, 96
 See also Bioko, 96
Fiennes, Sir Ranulph, 44, 45,
  46, 47, 48
 1970 Jostedalsbre
  Expedition, 45
 Mind Over Matter, 46
Foo, Mark, 212-214
Foucard, Charles de, 81
Franklin, Sir John, 1, 11, 130
Franz Josef Land (also Francis
  Joseph's Land), 15, 16
Frederick Jackson Island, 16
 See also Jackson Island
French, Eva & Francesca, 67-71
 Gobi Desert Expedition,
  1927, 67-71
French Flying Corps, 66
Fridtjof Nansen Mountain, 23
 See also Nansen, Mount
Fuchs, Sir Vivian, 39, 40, 41,
  42

Gagarin, Major Yuri
  Alexeyevich, 5, 227-230,
  239
 First human in space, 1961,
  227-230
Galdhoppigen, Noway, 178

Garwood, Edmund Johnston, 19
George V Coast, 28
See also King George V Land
Gharian mountains, Libya, 54
Gibson Desert, 86
Gill, Allan, 50, 51
Gobi Desert, 66
Gobi Desert expedition, 1927, 67-71
Grant, James, 125
Great Britain Air Race, The, 1912, 220-222
Great Fish River, 13
See also Back River
Greenland, 8, 9, 49, 50, 51, 201
Grit Ridge Glacier, 19
Guardian, The, 5

Haardt, GM, 65
1923 French expedition by car, 65-67
Habeler, Peter, 175
Haddo, Lord George Gordon, 135-138
Hadhramaut, 69, 73, 75
Haise, Fred, 236-238
Hall, Ron and Nicholas Tomalin, 203-207
The Strange Voyage of Donald Crowhurst, 203-207
Harbo, George 196
Harrison, Marguerite, 119, 121
Hedges, Kenneth, 50
Herbert, Sir Wally, 48
Obituary, 48-52
1961-1962 Southern Exploration
Herbert Plateau, 49
A World of Men, 50
1963: living with the Inuit
1968-9 British trans-Arctic expedition, 50
Herzog, Maurice 159-161
Annapurna, 159-161
See also Himalayas; French Himalayan Expedition
Heyerdahl, Thor 188-190, 200
The Kon-Tiki Expedition, 188-190
Hidden Peak, 177
Hillary, Sir Edmund, 3, 39, 41, 42, 162, 166, 170
Himalayas, 148-150, 167, 177
Annapurna, 159-161
Trisul, ascent of, 148, 149
Everest, Mount 148, 150-151, 153, 161
French Himalayan Expedition, 1950 159-161
Joseph Brown, 1955 167
Hindu Kush, 165
Horn, Dr Gunnar, 38
Norwegian scientific exploration of 1929, 38
Hudson, Charles, 135-138
Hunt, Sir John, 162, 166
Huntford, Roland, 42
Scott and Amundsen, p. 42

Ibn Rashid, 85
Ice Chimney, The, 174-175
See also Wilson, Maurice
India, 122
Indian Archipelago, 100
Indian army, 88
Indian Ocean, 57, 60
International Association of Women Explorers, The, 119, 120
Inuit, 11, 12, 49, 50
Iran, 111, 113
See also Persia
Iraq, 60, 61
Irvine, Sandy, 150-151
Islam, 63, 65, 84
Island of Montreal, 13
Istanbul Strait, 61
See also Bosphorous

Jackson, Frederick, 17
Jackson Island, 16
See also *Frederick Jackson Island*
Japan, 112
Jebel Shammar, Saudi Arabia, 85
Johansen, Hjalmer, 14
Johnson, Amy 4, 224-225
Solo flight to Australia of 1929, 224-225
Jordan, 81

Kanchenjunga, 169
Kashmir, 147
Kellas, Alexander Mitchell, 153
Kenyon Mackensie, Jean, 119
Khartoum, 125
Khazakstan, 68
King Haakon VII Plateau, 24
See also Antarctic Plateau
King George V Land, 28
King William's Island, 12
Kingsley, Mary 108-110
Knox-Johnston, Robin 202-203
Koerner, Roy, 50
Kropp, Göran 178-180
Obituary, 178-180
Kurds, 113

Lachenal, Louis, 160
Laing, Major Gordon, 53
Attempted expedition Tripoli to Timbuctoo, 1825 53-56
Murder of, 56
Landor, Savage, 139-142
Torture and imprisonment in Tibet, 1897, 139
Lawrence, TE, 82, 85
Layard, Austen Henry, 61
Lhasa, Tibet, 145, 146, 147, 152
Lhotse, Mount, 175
Libya, 54, 56
Lindbergh, Captain Charles, 4, 223-224
First flight across the Atlantic, 223-224
Livingstone, Dr David, 4, 90, 102, 105, 106, 116, 117
London Alpine Club, 135, 148
Longstaff, Dr Tom G, 148-150, 153
Lovell, Mary S 87-91
A Rage to Live: A Biography of Richard and Isabel Burton, 87-91
Lovell, Captain James, 236-238
Lundborg, Einar, 37
Lusar, Tibet, 144

Manchester Guardian, 27
MacArthur, Ellen, 210-211
Macarthy, Tim, 34
Ma'an, Jordan, 81
MacNish, Harry, 34, 35
Macquarie Island, 28
Malay Peninsula, 112
Malawi, Lake, 106, 107
  See also 'Lake N'Yassa'
Mali, 53-56, 80
Mallory, George, 1, 150-151
Matterhorn 135-138
  Fatal accident of 1865, 135-138
  Aiguille Sans Nom, 138-139
Matthews Shelby, Gertrude, 119
Mawson, Sir Douglas, 27
Mauna Loa, 112
Mauretania, 80
Mecca, 79, 85, 88
  Pilgrimmage, 82, 88
Mehringer, Karl, 157-159
Mekon, River, 94
  See also Mekong, River
Mekong, River, 94
  See also Mekon River
Messner, Reinhold, 175-178
  Oxygen free ascent of Everest 1978, 175
  Lhotse conquest, 1986 175-176
Milnes, Monckton MP, 90
Mirambo, King of Ujowa, 102, 103
Moorhouse, Geoffrey, 78-81
  Sahara Expedition, 78-81
  The Fearful Void, 78-81
Morocco, 79 84, 85, 88
Mouhot, Henri 93-99
  Travels in the Central Parts of Indo-China (Siam), Cambodia and Laos, during the years of 1858, 1859 and 1860 by the late M Henri Mouhot, 93-99
Mountain Review, 47
Mumm, A. L. 148-149

N'Yassa, Lake, 106
  See also 'Malawi, Lake'
Nanga Parbat, Mount 177
Nansen, Fridtjof, 14, 15, 16
  1893-96 expedition to North Pole, 14
Nansen, Mount, 23
Nepal, 160-164
New Siberia, 9
New Zealand, 111
New Zealand Antarctic Programme, 49
New York Herald, 102
Newby, Eric 165
  A Short Walk in the Hindu Kush, 165
Niger, River, 53
Nile, River, 80, 89, 107, 125, 126
Niles, Blair, 119, 120
Nobile, Umberto, 35, 36, 37
  Italia North Pole expedition, 35-38
North Pole, 11
  1818 expedition, 7, 8
  1893-96 expedition, 14
  polar basin, 8
  1929 *Italia* expedition, 35-37
  British Transarctic Expedition, 50
Norway, 17, 178
Nuristan Province, 165
  See also Hindu Kush; Afghanistan

Oates, Lawrence, 4, 45
Odell, Noel, 150-151
Oman, 69
Omsk, Siberia, 67, 68
Ottoman Empire, 61, 67, 84

Paccard, Dr Michel-Gabriel, 133-135
Palestine, 113
Palgrave, William Gifford, 76
Paulet Island, 31
Peary, Robert, 52
Pennines, The, 167
Persia, 111 , 113
  See also Iran
Persian Gulf, 69
Petra, Jordan 81
Philby, Harry St. John Bridger, 76
Piccard, Jacques 192
Pilatre de Rozier, Jean-Francois, 3
Pixton, Howard, 212
Point Ogle, 13
Polar Seas, 10, 11
Polo, Marco, 68, 82
Poole, James, 57
Polynesia, 188

Radiotelephone, 194, 195
Rae, Dr John 11
Rajah Brooke, 99
  See also Brooke, James
Ralston, Aron, 181-182
Rattin, Stephen, 124
Read, Piers Paul 171-173
  Alive: The Story of the Andes Survivors, 171-173
Ridgway, Captain John, 196-199
Rijnhart, Susie Carson144-145
  With the Tibetans in Tent and Temple, 144-145
Rocky Mountains, 112
Ross Sea, 28
Rovuma, River, 106
Royal Geographical Society, 51, 88, 90, 127, 146
Royal School of Military Survey, 48
Rub' al Khali, 68, 69, 76, 77, 78, 79
  See also Empty Quarter
Russell, Earl John, 96
Russia, 68

Sahara, 56, 65, 66, 76, 79
  French expedition by car, 1923, 65-67
  Kegresse-Hinstin caterpillar, 66
  Geoffrey Moorhouse Sahara Expedition, 78-81
Samarra, Iraq 60
Samuelson, Frank, 196
Sargasso Sea, 206
Saudi Arabia, 77, 85
Scoresby, William, 9
Scott, Captain Robert Falcon, 1, 2, 25, 39, 45, 46, 49
  Final expedition 1911, 25, 26, 28

Scott base, 41
Scott and Amundsen, Roland Huntford, 42-44
Sedlmayer, Max, 157-157
Seeley, Sir John Robert, 63
Semey, Kazakhstan 68
See also Semipalatinsk
Semipalatinsk, 68
See also Semey
Seton-Karr, Sir Henry122-123
Shackleton, Sir Ernest Henry, 24, 28, 29, 39, 40, 45, 49
Furthest point, 24
1914 expedition, 29- 35
Endurance, ship, sinking of 29-31
Shipton, Eric 153-156, 208
Nanda Devi, 153-156
Siam, 93
See also Thailand
Siberia, 38, 68
Sinai, 81
Singh, Nain, 146-147
Slave Trade, The, 95-99
Smithers, Leonard, 90
Sno-Cat, 40
South Georgia, 29, 34, 35
South Pole, 21, 49
1911 expedition, 21-25
Polheim, 25
Framheim, 25
Shackleton expedition, 1914, 29-35
South Ice British support base, 40
South Shetland Islands, 32
Speke, John Hanning, 89, 90, 125
Spitsbergen, 10, 15, 38
1897 expedition, 17, 18
Sputnik, 226
Stanhope, Lady Hester, 65
Stanley, Henry, 4, 102-108, 115, 117
Stark, Freya. 71-75
The Southern Gates of Arabia, 71-75
Stromness, 35
Whaling station, 35
Stroud, Dr Mike, 44, 45, 46, 47, 48
Shadows On The Wasteland, 45
Stuart, John McDouall, 57- 60
Central Mount Stuart, 59
Expedition Adelaide to shore of Indian Ocean, 57
Sturt, Captain Charles Napier, 57, 58, 59
Sudan, 54, 76, 125
Surfing, 211-215
Svalbard archipelago, 20, 51, 52
Svedrup, Otto, 50
Swigert, Jack, 236-238
Swinburne, Algernon, 90
Switzerland, 67
Syria, 62, 63, 64, 89, 113

Tanzania, 102-108, 115
Tehran, 111, 113
Telegraph, The, 164
Tensing, Sherpa Norgay, 162-164
See also Wangdi, Namgyal
Thailand, 93
See also Siam
Thesiger, Wilfred, 76-78
Arabian Sands, 76-78
Thomas, Bertram, 76
Tibet, 114, 139-142, 144-145, 152, 174
Tibesti Mountains, 76
Tilman, Major Harold William, 208-210
Timbuctoo, 53, 55, 56, 65
Times, The, 164
Tokyo, 112
Tomalin, Nicholas & Ron Hall 203-207
The Strange Voyage of Donald Crowhurst, 203-207
Tripoli, 53, 54, 55
Tuaric, the, 54 80
Tuat, the 55
Turkey, 63

Ukheidir, Iraq 60
United States, 5, 96, 235
See also America
Unyanyembe, Tanzania 102
Ujiji, Tanzania 102, 103, 105, 108, 115
Uruq al Shaiba, Saudi Arabia 77
Utah, 181

Valentine, James, 220
Vedrines, Jean Charles Toussaint, 220
Vincent, John, 34, 35
'Vinland', 202
Griffin 200-201

Wallace, Alfred Russell, 3, 99-102
The Malay Archipelago: the land of the Orang-utan, and the Bird of Paradise, 99-102
Walker, Colonel James, 145
Walsh, Lieutenant Don, 192-194
Wangdi, Namgyal, 162-164
See also Tensing, Sherpa Norgay
Ward, Herbert 115-118
A Voice from the Congo, Comprising Stories, Anecdotes and Descriptive Notes, 115-118
West Africa, 108
Webb, Captain Matthew, 183-185
Swimming the English Channel in 1875, 183-185
Weymann, Charles, 221
Whillans, Don, 169
Whimper, Edward 135-138
White Island, 38
Whitten-Brown, Sir Arthur 222
Flight Newfoundland to Ireland, 1919, 222
Wild, Frank, 33, 34
Wilder Lane, Rose, 119
Williams, Misha, 131-132
Wilson, Maurice, 174-175
Wiluna, Australia86
Worsley, Frank, 34, 35

Yangtze, River, 114
Yemen, 73, 74

Zambizi, River, 107
Zanzibar, 102, 106, 115, 125